William B. Carpenter

**On Sermon Preparation**

Recollections and Suggestions

William B. Carpenter

**On Sermon Preparation**
*Recollections and Suggestions*

ISBN/EAN: 9783337159917

Printed in Europe, USA, Canada, Australia, Japan

Cover: Foto ©Lupo / pixelio.de

More available books at **www.hansebooks.com**

ON
# SERMON PREPARATION

*RECOLLECTIONS AND SUGGESTIONS*

BY
THE BISHOP OF RIPON,
THE DEAN OF NORWICH, THE DEAN OF CANTERBURY,
ARCHDEACON SINCLAIR, CANON TRISTRAM,
PREBENDARY WEBB-PEPLOE, THE REV. H. C. G. MOULE,
THE REV. F. J. CHAVASSE, THE REV. W. H. M. H. AITKEN,
THE REV. A. J. HARRISON, THE REV. H. SUTTON,
AND THE REV. A. R. BUCKLAND

New York
MACMILLAN AND CO.
66 FIFTH AVENUE
1896

# NOTE

THE Authors of this volume were in each case invited to explain their own methods of Sermon Preparation. Whilst the advice they offer is for the most part applicable to any Sermon, the Rev. W. H. M. H. Aitken has dealt more especially with the Mission Sermon; the Rev. A. J. Harrison with the Evidential Sermon; Canon Tristram and the Rev. H. Sutton with the Missionary Deputation's Sermon. The articles were originally published in the columns of the *Record*.

# CONTENTS

|  | PAGE |
|---|---|
| INTRODUCTION. BY THE REV. A. R. BUCKLAND, M.A., MORNING PREACHER AT THE FOUNDLING HOSPITAL ... ... ... | 1 |
| I. BY THE RIGHT REV. W. BOYD CARPENTER, D.D., BISHOP OF RIPON ... ... | 15 |
| II. BY THE VERY REV. W. LEFROY, D.D., DEAN OF NORWICH ... ... ... | 32 |
| III. BY THE VERY REV. F. W. FARRAR, D.D., DEAN OF CANTERBURY ... ... ... | 49 |
| IV. BY THE VENERABLE W. M. SINCLAIR, D.D., ARCHDEACON OF LONDON ... ... | 60 |
| V. BY THE REV. H. B. TRISTRAM, D.D., F.R.S., CANON OF DURHAM ... ... ... | 82 |
| VI. BY THE REV. H. C. G. MOULE, D.D., PRINCIPAL OF RIDLEY HALL, CAMBRIDGE | 105 |
| VII. BY THE REV. F. J. CHAVASSE, M.A., PRINCIPAL OF WYCLIFFE HALL, OXFORD ... | 124 |

VIII. BY THE REV. H. W. WEBB-PEPLOE, M.A., VICAR OF ST. PAUL'S, ONSLOW SQUARE, AND PREBENDARY OF ST. PAUL'S CATHEDRAL ... ... ... ... ... 159

IX. BY THE REV. W. H. M. H. AITKEN, M.A., GENERAL SUPERINTENDENT OF THE CHURCH PAROCHIAL MISSION SOCIETY 174

X. BY THE REV. A. J. HARRISON, B.D., EVIDENTIAL MISSIONER OF THE CHURCH PAROCHIAL MISSION SOCIETY ... ... 188

XI. BY THE REV. H. SUTTON, M.A., VICAR OF ASTON, BIRMINGHAM ... ... ... 207

# ON SERMON PREPARATION

## INTRODUCTION

By the Rev. A. R. BUCKLAND, M.A.,
*Morning Preacher at the Foundling Hospital.*

THE ministry of the Church of England is probably the only one into which half its clergy enter without having received the most elementary advice upon the preparation and preaching of sermons. It is true that they may also be without the smallest experience of other duties into which they will presently be thrust. But these others are less public, and offer more opportunities for the mistakes of the novice to escape general comment. In the pulpit he appears as a teacher; and it is not meet that he should compel commiseration rather than the attention proper to interested hearers.

Yet no sooner has a young man of twenty-three been ordained than it is boldly assumed that he is competent to instruct from the pulpit the people of the parish to which he is licensed as a curate. He may never in his life have addressed ten people in a group; he may never, save for a Bishop's Examining Chaplains, have composed the simplest homily; he may be absolutely devoid of natural aptitude for speaking in public, or for putting his thoughts upon paper at his leisure. Nevertheless, if he satisfy the Bishop upon other points, he may, nay, he assuredly will, enter the pulpit to preach as soon as he has been ordained. A deacon, fresh from the hands of the Bishop of London, has been left in charge of a parish and all the services of the Church on the very Sunday after he was ordained. No doubt that was a scandal; but it is also an illustration of the way in which, because he has been ordained, a young man is presumed capable of exercising duties as trying as they are serious.

When one reflects upon the absence of, or the inadequacy of, training for the pulpit which the English clergy receive, it is an unceasing source of wonder that men should be as ready to "hear sermons" as they are. It is a simple matter for the cynic to answer, "They do not hear." No doubt there are now, and there always have been, preachers at whose first words the congregation compose themselves in attitudes that bespeak studied inattention to the pulpit. But these preachers are the exceptions. No doubt, too, many regular Churchgoers have become cruelly expert in keeping an aspect of serious attention whilst their thoughts are far away. But in the main I believe that at the beginning of the sermon people do give their attention, and that, even under sorest temptation, many continue it to the end.

Much of their patience may be due to habit. Certainly we may not always trace it to the sermons. It may positively be affirmed that if the sermon were a novelty proposed for the first time to be used in our churches it would utterly fail, in a large number of cases, to vindicate its right to live. No wonder that the Bishop of Liverpool[1] boldly declares that "the utter want of any proper training for the pulpit is one great blot and defect in the system of the

[1] *Simplicity in Teaching* (W. Hunt & Co.). Second Edition, 1884, p. 48.

Church of England." His own experience was that of countless clergy—"Nobody ever told me what was right or wrong in the pulpit. The result was that the first year of my preaching was a series of experiments." The people upon whom the experiments are made do not always fare as well as those who sat under the Rev. J. C. Ryle in 1841.

It is impossible not to contrast the light-hearted way in which capacity for preaching is now assumed with the greater care exercised at other periods in the Church's history. An early custom which confined preaching to the Bishop suggests a dignity and importance for the office which is at least better than the indolent assumption that qualifications are not worth inquiring into. To lack the gift conspicuously was held so serious as to discredit a Bishop. There was this further peculiarity, that in those days presbyters or deacons allowed to preach, were assumed to do so as the Bishop's representative. He was responsible for the views they expounded. It is well that the custom is gone. If it were proposed to subject a really able and sensitive Bishop to torture, perhaps nothing more exquisitely cruel could be devised than that he should hear week by week [all the sermons preached by the clergy in his name. In regard to this, however, it is but fair to remind ourselves that the effort of the Archbishop of York to spare both the younger clergy and their hearers by limiting their delivery of original sermons has ancient precedent. The delivery by deacons of recognized sermons by illustrious authors was a witness to the respect in which the sermon was held by the early Church, and to the presence of some of the very difficulties we are sensible of to-day.

It may be argued, perhaps, that the Churchman's attitude towards the sermon is the natural outcome of the modern view of clerical duty. It is inevitable that Nonconformity should set preaching first amongst ministerial qualifications; it is equally inevitable that in the Church we should think first of the parish. In the effort, however, to obtain clergy who will be equally competent in the pulpit and out of it; equally devoted to the drudgery of parish work as to more public duties; equally happy by the bedside of the sick, at the working-men's club, and in the pulpit, we face the certainty of finding some qualities deficient. Nay, more; the ever-increasing extent and variety of the duties demanded from the clergy, coupled with the disposition to develop worship on its sensuous side, make it impossible that the average clergyman should deal fairly with his sermon. He is sorely tempted to starve one part of his ministerial work for the sake of the other. Is he an able preacher? Pressed to go hither and thither, conscious that his words are watched and discussed, conscious also that he has been of use at least to some, he may relax his hold upon other work, leaving it to other hands under his control. Is he a skilful organizer, administrator, or toiler in the less public work of the ministry? Then, happy in his individual tasks and in the cares of organization, aware of a certain incapacity in the pulpit, he may neglect that side of his work from very despair of much usefulness in it. Some, remarking the sorrows of men who feel deeply their unfaithfulness to one part or the other of their duties, have proposed a Preaching Order, for the relief alike of such as have no pulpit gifts and of such as, having them, are happy in no other work.

But it might also be affirmed that the conventional assumption that every ordained person is qualified to preach is a mark of the honour in which preaching is held. And indeed the sermon has just claim to reverence. No great movement in the Church has ever succeeded without its aid. The Reformation alike in England and on the Continent, from the efforts of Wiclif's "poor priests" onwards, owed its influence over the people very largely to its use of the sermon. The Evangelical Revival was emphatically the work, on its human side, of preachers. In the history of the Oxford Movement stages are marked by sermons, and its leaders laid themselves out to reach the people through the pulpits of the land. The influence of the modern Broad Church School in England is largely due to the fact that it has possessed men who had and have the ear of the people. Nor are there any signs that the religious forces of the age regard the sermon as obsolete. Year by year the number of sermons grows, and though no one would venture to say that in quality they everywhere improve, yet in feeling and in earnestness they are, in the main, far beyond the theological abstractions and the dull moralizing which over and over again have been almost supreme.

There are deficiencies, no doubt, but are they

not the deficiencies of all time? The sermon is a human instrument, in which the defects of the human preacher are certain to be manifest, however deep his spirituality, however intense his earnestness. There are those who, having stated their text and expounded it more or less briefly, depart into applications, reflections, exhortations, bound by only the slenderest cord of thought to the truth or incident from which they start. It is charged against them as an error; but so erred Chrysostom and many others before them. They may be numbered as the men who, earnestly seeking to interpret life by the light of Holy Scripture, unconsciously use that light all too sparingly. Their peril is that, in dealing with life around them, they may neglect the one constant quantity in the Apostolic sermon, the preaching of Christ Himself and Him crucified.

Are some mystical, allegorizing to the last stretch of their hearers' patience—or even beyond? Even so did Origen, Ambrose, and many more before them. They have not made men irreverent. They have not ministered to neglect of Holy Scripture. They have not countenanced that view of the Bible narratives which refuses to see any meaning beyond the plainest historical statement or the simplest moral teaching.

Have some fallen into the peril of the anecdote-monger, calling to their aid the pretty stories of child literature and some others more adapted to developed intelligence? So also did the Dominicans and Franciscans of the Middle Ages, and many heard them with profit. They at least won, and still win, hearers who require milk as babes, and with this may also have "the sincere milk of the Word."

Have some been led to preach in terms that approach the intellect rather than the heart, to deal in subtleties, and surround the pulpit with the atmosphere of the schools? So also did Thomas Aquinas before them. If some depart in haste from their neighbourhood, others remain who would not remain elsewhere.

Have some expressed themselves in language tender, pathetic, dreamy; full of aspirations after holiness, breathing a spirit of aloofness from the world, speaking to the conscience of men in a mood of exaltation? So preached Tauler and the Mystics before them, and moved such hearts as that of Luther himself.

Nay, greater faults—if faults they be—than these find their counterpart in bygone days. There are men who begin, as it were, in a far country, and presently roam back, by more or less devious paths, in the direction of their texts. There are men who commit themselves to distant wanderings; who make some to wish that they might intervene, as Elizabeth did when at untimely words on female vanity she bade one "Leave that ungodly digression and return to" his text. They abounded in pre-Reformation days.

There are men who taste a scarcely concealed joy in announcing texts from little read portions of the Bible, or texts which suggest a topical allusion, however remote that allusion may be from the true import of the scriptural passage. They have had their predecessors in all ages. They reflect with complacency upon the Puritan who preached from "Nine-and-twenty knives" (Ezra i. 9), and the contemporary who expanded "Aha, aha" (Psalm lxx. 3). They accept as legitimate Hook's use of "Hear the Church" (Matt. xviii. 17) as the text for a sermon on obedience to ecclesiastical authority; and as equally legitimate Whately's suggestion for a corrective sermon from the fuller text, "If he neglect to hear the Church, let him." They deem peculiarly appropriate the Dominican's text against Galileo and his friends, "Ye men of Galilee, why stand ye gazing up into heaven?" They would, if occasion arose, preach another cholera sermon, with Dean Buckland, from the text, "Wash and be clean."

Are some rhetorical and vain-glorious? So also were many in Jerome's day. "The simplicity and purity of Apostolic language is neglected," he wrote; "we meet as if we were in the Athenæum or the lecture-rooms, to kindle the applause of the bystanders; what is now required is a discourse painted and tricked out with spurious rhetorical skill, and which, like a trumpet in the street, does not aim at instructing the public but at winning their favour."

There are some who miss sorely the applause proper to the platform, and once common in church. They reflect that they would not have followed Chrysostom and Augustine in reproving their hearers for showing approval thus. They would even accept the modern substitute for such applause, permitted in some quarters, the groan of deeply moved assent or the stimulating presence of a hearty "Amen." Failing these, they do not disdain to elicit a cheerful smile amongst their hearers. The same disposition to stimulate attention by quips was familiar in pre-Reformation times.

Are there some who love to magnify the incidentals of the scriptural narrative; who dwell with infinite care upon the suggested meanings of the word spikenard, the composition of the precious unguent and its probable cost per pound, and the spiritual lessons suggested by it; who can discover explicit statements of the Gospel in every incident of Israel's wanderings and in every part of the High Priest's clothing? They have been forestalled.

Are there some who, under pressure of other work, and the stress of a ministry continued for too many years in one parish, feel that they have exhausted themselves, and fall back for relief upon ready-made sermons? They could count an ample array of precedent, including one volume bearing the ominous title of *Dormi Secure*.

Are some affected by the size and attention of their congregation? So also was Gregory of

Nyssa, who declared that when he saw the flock gathered round him he worked "with pleasure" at his sermons, "as the shepherds do at their rustic strains," but when things were otherwise was "much troubled and glad to be silent."

Are some given to long sermons—so that they might say with Barrow, when asked whether his Spital sermon of three hours and a half had not wearied him, "Yes, indeed, I begin to be weary in standing so long"? They have had many predecessors.

But every preacher whose heart is in his work is conscious of shortcomings. He falls below his own desires; he feels that, with better opportunities, he might perform his task better. The methods of the great preachers of the past, so far as they are known to us, have always varied. Occasionally, no doubt, the facts differ widely from the received opinions amongst the general public. It has been assumed, for example, by some that the late Canon Liddon spent the intervals during which he was not in residence, in the elaborate preparation of his St. Paul's sermons. This assuredly was not the case. The remarkable felicity of his language was not the result of special care but equally marked the expression of his ideas in the most ordinary conversation. Canon Liddon at the height of his fame had amassed immense stores of knowledge which were completely under command. He drew upon them at will; and it is probable, therefore, that his own methods of sermon preparation differed widely from that which he suggests in *The Priest in his Inner Life*. In no department of a clergyman's work is it more unlikely that any one set of rules could apply with advantage to all. Men differ in knowledge of the Bible, in knowledge of self, in knowledge of other men; in temperament as well as in knowledge; in spirituality also, and in the realization of the responsibility which attaches to all their work. But where men would shrink from imposing laws they may readily lend advice. Such advice some of the foremost of our English preachers offer in the series of chapters to which this is introductory.

# I

By the RIGHT REV. W. BOYD CARPENTER, D.D.,
*Bishop of Ripon.*

THE preparation for the pulpit is twofold. There is a preparation which is conscious and deliberate. There is a preparation which is unconscious, which is the product of all a man's previous study, reading, and habits of thought. Both these kinds of preparation need attention.

I.—There is the direct preparation. By this, I mean, of course, the preparation which is consciously and deliberately given to the making of the sermon. This implies the choice of the subject —its arrangement—its expression.

Choice of subject.—This is sometimes a very difficult matter. We may choose some favourite text; and so far this is easy. But, after a time, the favourite texts are exhausted. We may adopt the plan of hunting for striking texts; but the temptation here is to detach text from context, and so preach not on the text but away from it. We may follow another custom. We may let the Church choose our text for us. In other words we may preach on the subject which the Church services suggest. There is much to be said for this plan, especially in the earlier years of our ministry. It introduces into our method a gentle compulsion which saves us from the one-sided selection of a few favourite themes. But it does not abolish all difficulty, for it is not always possible to repeat this plan year after year, and even here we must exercise choice; for we must determine whether Epistle or Gospel or Lesson is to yield us our text.

The truth is that in every method there is difficulty. But let not difficulty deter us; and never let this difficulty of choice drive us away from our own responsibility and duty into the bad habit of depending on other men's sermons. I knew of one preacher whose habit it was to read some good sermon first, and then prepare his own on the same subject. This seems to me to be a perilous and doubtful experiment. It is likely to put memory to work rather than thought; and so far as it does this, it may make you stronger to-day at the cost of making you weaker afterwards. Intellectual stimulants of this kind are as harmful in their way as stimulants of another kind. In both cases they are the confession of weakness.

The truth is that the harder way is often the easier one in the end. What is grown takes a longer time to reach maturity than what is made; but the best things grow. The best sermons among other things. The reason is simple. What grows partakes of the very nature of that out of which it grows. The sermon which grows is one in which a part of ourselves goes out; and the sermon ought to be the outcome of our own life and experience. No text, therefore, should be chosen except such as voices truths which are true to us. For we must be the mouthpieces not only of truth, but of truth which we know and feel to be true. It will be said, "This will limit our choice of texts. Will it not also be the same as throwing us back on our favourite texts?" I think not. The truths in the Bible are very few, and yet very great. There are certain principles which appear and reappear. The same truth expresses itself in history, in parable, in aphorism, in poetry, in argument, and in dogmatic statement.

If the truth be one which has become ours, realized so clearly and embraced so strongly that we can delight in it, feed on it, then we shall rejoice in teaching and tracing it as it emerges out of story, treatise, and song; in the lips of Psalmist, historian, and Apostle. In order that our grasp on these principles may be a real, personal, and strengthening grasp, there must be much personal reading, meditation, and prayer. But this belongs to the subject of indirect preparation, which will come later. For the present I only wish to say that, in the long run, the hard path of daily and persevering personal study of the Bible will make the choice of texts, instead of a difficulty, a joy; for the spirit will have reaped from the abundance of truth, and out of that abundance the heart will speak.

If we carry this habit of study and thought into every service and every duty, we shall find that material will accumulate. Suggestions for sermons will be constantly arising. The texts will be ready beforehand. The anxiety of Saturday will be an unknown thing. You will not need to go about city or study hunting for a text.

To give practical value to this habit of study

and thought, it is well to have a note-book into which to enter the subjects and lines of thought for sermons as they arise. There will, no doubt, be many such outlines which will never be used, but the practice of noting them down will be of service. It will keep the mind fresh and full; it will also prevent that hasty and raw making up of sermons which can hardly be called preparation at all. You will have subjects in hand long before they are wanted. Advent, Lent, Christmas, Easter, Whitsuntide will have themes ready beforehand. The burden of choice will disappear, if we so keep ourselves to that dutiful and constant study which accumulates treasure, and if we cultivate that freshness and watchfulness of mind which can bring out of that treasure things new and old.

The arrangement of a subject is only second in importance to its selection. Order is the sermon's first law as well as nature's. Let us grudge no time spent upon discovering the fittest order for our subject. And for this purpose, let us remember that our duty is to persuade men. We must not irritate their understandings by needless circumlocution or perplexing deviations from our line of thought. There are some preachers who run up to their subject only to run away from it again. They are like birds who hop about a morsel of bread—eye it doubtfully and then beat a hasty retreat—only to reappear again and repeat the same manœuvre.

The reason of this hesitation is that the preacher has not made up his mind either as to his subject or to the order in which he can approach it. This is the reason why sermons so often lack grip. What is said is good and true, but it fails to lay hold upon the mind of the hearer, because the preacher has failed to grasp his own subject. It is indispensable that the preacher should see his sermon from end to end; that the lines before him should be clear, intelligible, and manageable lines. He must know where he means to stop as well as where he means to begin. For that time is not lost which is spent in securing the order of his sermon. To secure it he must reject much which is attractive, if in any way it leads him astray from his main purpose; and his purpose should be clear throughout his discourse. It is not of so much importance whether the structure of his sermon be analytical or synthetic so long as the structure is a real one. In other words it must not be a collection of ideas, but an assemblage of thoughts which cohere together, and arise out of one another. The mind of the hearer is then carried on from point to point, and each portion tends to strengthen the main argument.

One or two hints on this subject may perhaps be useful. Let the order be from the simplest thoughts to the less simple. Let your first utterance be that which all can understand; make clear your subject. If it depend upon some Bible narrative, present the narrative to your hearers. Simplicity is the best commencement; fire, according to the French axiom, "fire in the exordium is fire in straw." We have heard some sermons which commenced promising eloquence, but which grew dull towards the close. The reason of this is that the preacher has been a little enamoured with some pet thought, but has lacked determination or patience to work out the whole subject in orderly fashion. His energy has spent itself in the introduction. Such a sermon might probably have been transformed by a very little trouble into a useful one, and one which would have sustained interest to the last. But it needed that its form should be recast.

Again, for this purpose think over your subject; observe its bearings on the life of men; consider how its principles will touch men of varying occupations; think of its relationship to the consciences you wish to touch, and lay your plans to reach the conscience and to enlist the heart.

Thirdly, the expression of the sermon must be considered. The text has been chosen; the order has been decided on; the subject must now be expressed to the people. How is this to be done? It may be written out and read; it may be written out, learned by heart, and delivered; or the subject in its matured order may be meditated upon, made part of ourselves; and then spoken out freely and simply to our audience. Of these three methods the first and the last are each good in their way. The second need be mentioned only to be condemned. It secures the advantages neither of the written sermon nor of the spoken one. The mind is not free as it is in the case of the spoken sermon, for the memory is put to a strain at the very moment when the mind should be in possession of its unfettered strength. There is truth in the saying that good speaking is thinking on your legs. The good speaker is the man who, though he is fully familiar with his subject, understands the order in which he intends to present it, and who, though bound by its order, yet speaks with a free and undistracted mind. He is a man who, notwithstanding that careful preparation which he has made, can fling his soul into what he says. The mere memoriter preacher can never do this. The sense that his memory is weighted makes him timid; the slip of a word, the failure of memory for a single moment may throw him off his balance. Moreover the fact that he has to deliver something from memory gives an air of unreality to what he says. He is so obviously dependent on his memory that his speech does not seem to come from his heart. In other words, his self-consciousness is provoked by the necessity of using his memory, and he cannot reach that self-abandonment which is essential to all effective extempore speaking.

The first plan of writing and reading a sermon has its advantages. Much anxiety of mind is spared; sleepless nights are often avoided. The practice can never be condemned as long as the names of Chalmers, and Melvill, and Liddon are remembered. But it still needs to be said that it is not every one who can read his written sermon as these men read theirs. Too often the monotonous reading, the downcast face, the closed throat which are the accompaniments of such a sermon, render it less effective than the less gracefully phrased spoken sermon. And certainly a political orator would hardly succeed if he were bound to his book. To face the people; to meet them with eye and voice; to be full of the earnest desire to persuade them to think as you think; to have something, well studied, much believed in, which you desire to make them believe also, and to be able simply and earnestly to give expression to your thoughts, is, on the whole, the shortest and simplest route to the hearts of men.

But whatever course is pursued it is indispensable that we should be earnest not merely when we are preparing our sermon, but when we are delivering it.

II.—This leads us to the other branch of our subject—the indirect preparation of the sermon. If a man's studies week by week are for his Sunday sermons only, he will be more like the lawyer getting up his brief than like the preacher delivering his soul. He makes direct preparation only. The indirect preparation is the personal study, reading, meditation, and prayer which is undertaken without thought of the Sunday sermon. In this personal study the man's mind grows riper and stronger for his ministry; he accumulates material without feeling that it is accumulated for a special purpose. He reads and makes his own what he reads. He becomes a richer and fuller man; and to that extent he is readier to commence the direct preparation for the sermon than he otherwise would be. In order to be fitly and fully prepared for preaching we should keep up a constant system of study which is independent of all direct preparation for the pulpit. One of the ablest preachers I ever knew made this an absolute rule. When he was asked how it was possible to find time for more than the reading needful for preaching, he said, " I must have it, even if I were to leave the special reading undone."

But this indirect preparation goes beyond reading. It is that self-preparation which means self-examination, personal piety, spiritual growth. These need their share of attention. Above all else the ethical quality of the man is of the first importance in preaching. The preacher should be a man of heavenly spirit ; he should not merely be a man who knows he has something to say ; he should be a man whose speech is out of the fulness of his heart. Such a man will be above the petty ambition of producing eloquent sermons and adorning them with tawdry ornaments ; he will be less and less rhetorical as he is more and more earnest. He may be an orator, for earnestness is indispensable to true oratory ; he certainly will speak effectively, because no man who earnestly desires to speak the truth, and takes pains to speak it simply and clearly, can fail to be effective. The range of his effectiveness may be less or more, but the reality of it will be undoubted. Such a man will know that the real object which he has in view is to touch the moral nature of his hearers. He will realize that the great force of the Gospel is its moral force. And whether we consider the direct or indirect preparation of sermons, this moral force of the Gospel must never be forgotten, lest the sermon should miss its mark.

III.—We need, therefore, to consider the relation of preaching to the conscience. It has an influence in the spheres of intellect, taste, politics ; but these are subordinate, the results of the overflow of its abounding power; they are not of its immediate intention, which is to touch, renew, elevate the moral nature of man. Its appeal is therefore to the conscience, and it is of immense advantage to the preacher that the tribunal before which he has to plead with man, on his own behalf, is that, not of the intellect, or the passion, or the tastes, but that of the conscience, because it is a tribunal which is guided by a simpler and more universal code than the intricate and contradictory standards of judgment, affection, and refinement; he can evoke a wider response, for with all the varieties of taste, education, attainments, race, class, and climate, he will find a more universal and unanimous verdict on moral questions than on others. Apart from the impulse of partiality and passion, there will be found a very general agreement when a simple question of right and wrong is laid before the public mind. Happy are we that we are not called to deal with vexed questions of philosophy, or widely contested opinions in metaphysics, but with broad issues of moral good and evil, where our duty is to commend ourselves to every man's conscience in the fear of God.

But how to reach this conscience? Our work may have an element of simplicity in being one which avoids certain erratic speculations; but this very simplicity is a source of difficulty on account of the variety, the eccentricity, and the number of attachments with which men have conspired to bar up every avenue by which the conscience may be approached. If the conscience is chief minister to the will, how can we secure an audience—where the vestibules and saloons are crowded with a throng of suppliants, and the throne-room occupied with a bevy of favourites and advisers? Where every caprice, every passion, every new fanciful thought or opinion sends its representative to dazzle, to oppress, or to fascinate the ruling power—where the rightful authority is set at nought, and every hour some new favourite monopolizes the monarch's ear—how can we make ourselves heard?

Like ambassadors, we shall be wise to understand the customs of the court, lest unwittingly we should lose our chance of an audience by breaking its harmless forms. If we would pierce into the presence-chamber, and hold converse with man's conscience, we must know somewhat of the nature of man, and of the causes which impede our approach. And it is not always easy to reach the conscience. "Every part of the duty of the minister of religion is more easy than to maintain in vigour the spirit which is needed as a reprover of sin, and a guardian of virtue."

I think Isaac Taylor was right when he wrote this; for when we consider the position which preaching occupies in our social system, the weakness of our own hearts, the vanity and exacting character of our hearers, we must feel at once that there are combined influences at work to enervate the vigour of our ministry to the consciences of men. As week after week rolls by, and Sunday after Sunday comes—when, more especially after the lapse of years, incessant labour has withered somewhat the freshness of our materials, there comes the temptation—the tendency to suffer the sermon to dwindle into a source of pleasure, or mere instruction—and to forget that the preaching of the Gospel is a great power for dealing with man's moral nature, and that every sermon which fails of this end is, as far as the immediate object of preaching is concerned, lost.

We must, therefore, realize that our object as

preachers of the Gospel is to reach the consciences of men; that though without this we may have pleased the more cultivated of our hearers and perplexed the more lowly, we have in reality accomplished nothing. We may have unfolded truth, we may have arrayed it in ornaments enchanting and attractive, but in manifesting truth we have failed to reach the conscience.

Two things are needed here—we need clear and strong personal convictions of truth and right. We must, that is, vividly realize the principles of God's government. We must not go after little things, or erect trifling customs or habits into serious sins. It confuses the conscience when matters of opinion and personal feeling are treated as though they were matters of grave moral importance. We must grasp clearly and set forth firmly two great principles of duty—love to God and love to man. To these the conscience will respond. In the next place we must do all this as guided by love. The conscience may make a man tremble; but it is only love that can fully work repentance. We are men seeking for men. The hands which are stretched out should be brotherly hands. Our Master's example will guide us. Even when He reproached the cities which had been unrepentant under His ministry, His love broke forth into the yearning cry, "Come unto Me, all ye that are weary and heavy laden." To be animated by this spirit is to possess the key to man's heart and conscience. The Spirit of Christ is the preacher's first and last need.

# II

By the VERY REV. WILLIAM LEFROY, D.D.,
*Dean of Norwich.*

IN treating of sermon preparation, I crave indulgence for the place which the personal element must necessarily occupy. My mode of this branch of work will be best understood by the method which lay behind it or beneath it. By this I mean the way in which from my earliest ministerial life I mapped out my time. For years, in Liverpool, I arose at five a.m. The seasons made no difference in this. My work began at about a quarter to six. It consisted of the Greek Testament and Theology. By nine o'clock I had three hours' reading, thinking, and notifying done. In this work Clark's Foreign Theological Library was to me invaluable. I always had a small book by my side, in which I jotted down texts which struck me, and I frequently turned to my Calendar to see on what day the chapter in which such a text was found occurred in the ordered Lesson, and if it were a Sunday I transcribed the text in a larger diary, making a note in it of the line of thought which was suggested, and for that sermon on such a Sunday my text was found and fixed. From that I seldom diverged.

From nine o'clock till ten was given to family prayer, breakfast, and the clearing of the morning correspondence. By that time I became liable to interruptions—serious, frivolous, irrelevant, musical, educational, parochial, domestic, financial. They had all one thing in common. They were vexatious, and I soon saw that, if I allowed it, they would absorb all the time I had saved between six and nine. I accordingly had a large and attractively printed card, neatly framed and glazed, hung in my hall, and so hung that it was, except the face of the servant, the first object that met a visitor's eye. It bore the following inscription :— " Rev. W. Lefroy engaged till 2.15 p.m." Many a wrangle occurred at that door. But the servant had her instructions, which were not on the card. My wife saw those who could not come at my appointed hour, or who had such business as she could arrange with me or without me. There were, too, cases which being exceptional in their character required exceptional treatment. But the restriction soon became known, and people were good enough to recognize its reasonableness. They learned, in one way or another, that when a student is at work he is entitled, if he can arrange it, to quiet and to freedom from disturbance. What a darkened chamber is to a photographer a library ought to be to a student. I have the strongest conviction that many a mental picture, with its background of Scripture, of history, of philosophy, and with its foreground of life, of perplexity, of religion, is ruined by a single tap at the door. There are times when great principles rise and grow, and revolve in the mind; when they seem, with the rapidity of a flash of lightning, to explain a hundred enigmas, to include a thousand facts, and to encircle ages of conflict, in preparation, in collision, in the progress of one idea, in the collapse of another. All this mental work is dashed by Mrs. Growler coming to inquire if Tommy Growler's school fees may not be paid for a fortnight! True, the interruption may have saved the congregation from much. But, however that may be, the student and his work are the first consideration.

Hence my hall notice. Hence to this hour, in this deanery, the perpetuation of it. Hence, too, my plea with my younger brethren, for deliberate, resolute, uninterrupted study. Nothing, save the cry of the sick or the dying, should be allowed to interfere with a clergyman engaged in study.

Moreover, the best book on each subject should be read. A good index enhances the value of every volume. The divisions of a book should be most carefully noted, and for myself I have always avoided divisions in a sermon, just as I shun the words "in conclusion." The use of these words arouses expectancy, impatience, and unrest in thousands of hearers.

I have said above that texts were frequently selected out of my early morning reading. This mode was but partial. The habitual and normal method, ever pursued in the early years of my Liverpool ministry, was otherwise. They were selected on Sunday night, and very often from the appointed lessons, or Epistle, or Gospel, or Psalms for the day. However worn by care, by exhaustion, by mental or moral expenditure, I seldom rested until I had, aided by entries made in my Lett, selected both texts for the following Sunday. This done, each Sunday evening for years I read Frances Ridley Havergal's most touching and comforting poem "Sunday Night." Many a time I fell asleep ere its soothing syllables were finished. But it was to me such a glimpse of the Master! He was near me, for I needed Him. And I have thanked Him that He ever allowed the author of that poem to live.

On Monday morning I regularly saw my curate. Amongst the subjects of our conversation, which I always jotted down as our agenda, were the books he was reading and the sermons he was to preach. In both I took the keenest interest. And as to the latter, he had ample time for preparation, and very often as much as a month's notice. The rest of Monday I gave to amusement. Passionately fond of exercise, I used to walk from Seacome Ferry to Leasowe Lighthouse along the sand and home by the high-road. Monday night brought me all that was lacking on Sunday night in the way of sleep. Then on Tuesday, at ten, I began to map out the sermon from the text which had been selected, either from the early morning reading or upon the Sunday night before.

This was sometimes done very rapidly and

sometimes very slowly. The difference depended upon the nature of the text and the varying method of treatment. If a text was doctrinal, such as Exod. xii. 13 ; Isa. liii. 4, 5, or 6; Ps. l. 5 or 21 ; Matt. iii. 17, xx. 28; Acts iii. 16; Eph. ii. 8, the work was direct. It was there on the surface of the passage. It was capable of being made of absorbing interest to every hearer by dealing with it theologically, that is, by showing the varied shades of truth or of falsehood, which had in days gone by, or in our own time, gathered round the doctrine revealed in the text. In this way, I am not conscious of ever having preached a doctrinal sermon without dealing with the doctrine with which that in the text stood in either designed or incidental or historical contrast. This compelled me, if I needed compulsion, to keep up my reading and to be vigilant in observation. It gave me, at all events, perpetual interest in my work. It gave freshness to well-worn themes. The heresies of pre-Reformation times and the defects and excesses of Nonconformity were dealt with. It enabled me to appeal to the Prayer-book, in the way of elucidation, confirmation, or warning. It showed my people the Scripturalness of our communion. It gave them a firm grasp of doctrine. Doctrinal sermons should ever include references to doctrinal exaggerations or defects.

The mapping out of these sermons, and about a page and a half of their expansion into composition was completed by one o'clock on Tuesday. Then I had luncheon, and at 1.15 till 2.15, accompanied by a large Irish retriever, I went to walk. That dog had many merits, but his conspicuous virtue was to assail, with vehemence, any one who attempted to converse with his master. For a good hour we chased over fields in Liverpool, which are now covered in by thousands of houses. At 2.15 I went to the schools; then I visited from house to house, returning to dine at 6.30. By 7.30 I was out to meetings of the usual parochial character, making for home by 10. On Wednesday, at 10 a.m., I resumed my composition of the Sunday evening's sermon, and continued it till 12. The same may be said of Thursday, and of Friday, by which day at 12 generally my Sunday evening's sermon, into which my strength, such as it was, was put, was finished. The hours saved on these days between 12 and 1.15 were given to literature, as were those of any evening in home.

But there were other than doctrinal sermons. There were ethical, topical, moral themes. These had ever to me a great attraction. They seemed to cover an immense area, in life, in suffering, in sorrow, and in sin; in action of all kinds. They admitted of variety of treatment, while they were capable of being applied to every man's character with the most clinging closeness. Such themes, arising out of the texts which contain them, are as much doctrinal as those I have cited. But these differ from those in not being revelations of the personal Christ, nor expressions of historicity. These texts contain great and pregnant principles. They assert the prevalence of laws, which govern the ages and those who exist in them. I refer now to such texts as Gen. xviii. 25, as revealing man's moral sense reposing upon his innate conviction of the final rectitude of Divine administration; or to Num. xxii. 9, showing God's observance of our associates; or Num. xxii. 12, 19, 20, 22, teaching that God may bestow in anger what He refuses in love; or Ezek. xviii. 2, the innocent suffering for the guilty; or St. John ix. 3, the

Divine mission of suffering; or Gal. vi. 7, every man his own outgrowth. Such texts as these—and they are selected as rapidly as the pen runs—admit of a different treatment from that to which the others are subject. These can be examined and analysed until we get back to the philosophic principle on which they rest and of which they are the voice and expression. I do not forget that others would treat them otherwise; but may I say that my method was to press behind all details, and to grasp the fundamental idea on which the precept or the principle rested. This having been gained, I began to search for its appearance, operation, recognition, or violation. I sought for it in individual, social, moral, political, or religious life. Every department of human interest was laid under contribution and pressed into service, and in the working out of my principle I was often impressed by the unity of truth amid the infinite variety which marked those who held it in different modes, ages, conditions.

One result of this sort of preaching was a considerable variety of vocabulary. Another was the unity which ran through the sermon. A third was the possibility of remembering it with ease, and the certainty that that sermon which is most orderly in arrangement is most easily remembered by both preacher and hearers. Such a sermon had but one idea, yet it would have many thoughts, and if well worked out it could be intelligently and aptly described; indeed, a name might be given to it. The late Archbishop Magee was Dean of Cork when I went to that city to begin my ministry. The Dean was most kind and helpful to me in the work of preaching. "My dear Lefroy," said the Dean to me when I was hesitating about the work of preaching as one reason for declining the incumbency of St. Andrew's, Liverpool, "master your subject, rule No. 1; master yourself, rule No. 2; put one idea into your sermon and as many thoughts as you can, and after you have worked that idea out you ought to be able to give your sermon a name. Unless you can it is a bad sermon." I adopted this plan for certainly the first ten years of my work in Liverpool.

I come now to a portion of the preparation about which I have found many men most reticent. I refer to what is known as memoriter delivery. I had made up my mind long before I was ordained that I would be, for better, for worse, an extempore preacher. For fifteen months after my appointment to Liverpool I used my MS., making it my servant in the most real sense, but resolved to be independent of it fully and finally. Accordingly, for years, I spent from 6 a.m. till 9 a.m. every Saturday morning in committing my Sunday evening sermon to memory, and as I continued this practice I soon became enabled to perfect this work in, say, two instead of three hours. Meanwhile the morning sermon had to be prepared, and the time at my disposal for this was between ten and one on Saturday. As a rule this sermon was purely expository. My steady and methodical reading helped me, while the careful drill of the composition for the evening sermon told in another way. It secured order in arrangement; it enlarged my vocabulary; it gave me wider and broader grasp of truth. In the mornings at St. Andrew's we had, as every one has, a family congregation. Our own people were present. They came for teaching, and we studied, in the way of exposition, the Pentateuch, Joshua, Judges, Jonah, the Epistles to the Galatians, Colossians, Philippians, and Romans.

## ON SERMON PREPARATION 43

As I gained freedom of utterance, and such clearness of diction as God in His mercy has bestowed upon me, I gradually gave up memoriter delivery; and while I never preach without having made full and careful preparation in very elaborate notes, most painfully ordered and wrought out, yet I never now resort to memoriter address. This I have not done for years. My early Liverpool Sunday evening sermons helped me to deliver my early Liverpool Sunday morning expositions. These latter in time delivered me from the memoriter mode, which, with its undoubted advantages, was yet slavish, wearing, and provocative of insomnia. It was distressing in the dead of night to remember one's forgets. In expository preaching it is most helpful to the hearers for the preacher to wait until they have found the text to which he refers. In extempore preaching when great principles or doctrines are being treated, the Holy Scripture should be cited and spoken memoriter. And he who presses art into this most sacred service will be careful to understand the meaning and the value of a pause, the management of the breath, the closing of the mouth at the end of a passage, and the inhaling of air through the nostrils, while he will avoid every approach to affectation, self-consciousness, and unreality.

Looking back over thirty years of very severe work in the ministry, I can truly say I have never prepared a sermon at night, or even in the evening. Of midnight oil I know nothing, absolutely nothing. Even now my rule is to prepare one sermon a week. When a curate in Cork this was then my rule. After fifteen months in my only curacy, I was appointed to St. Andrew's, Liverpool. My stock of sermons was twelve which I had preached, and some forty which have never been preached. I have now thirty-three books of notes of sermons, and a pile of manuscript representing my earlier efforts in Liverpool. I never even look at the latter. And unless sorely driven, seldom use any of the former. It would not cost me five minutes' concern if some little dog Diamond consigned my sheets to the flames.

I have some very strong persuasions about preaching. One of them is the mortification I have felt that sometimes a subject of commanding importance was less carefully treated than it might be, through causes which, however I tried to guard against them, were within my own control.

It is, let me assure my junior brethren, maddening to feel as you are preaching God's truth that your message might have been better prepared. Another is the humiliation I have experienced, again and again, that sermons over which I have laboured for even fifteen hours, have fallen dead as lead upon my hearers, when a simple exposition has interested, informed, and edified them. A third is, that I have never been as happy after a sermon as when I preached my Master in the sermon. This is the one fact about which I have no regret. And, without referring more exactly to the sacred and secret side of sermon preparation, may I say this one word? I have again and again stood in my pulpit in St. Andrew's, Liverpool, with a fluttering heart, excited nerves, throbbing brain, and racking headache. I have wondered how the sermon would be delivered. But I have looked at that crowd of expectant souls. The reflection arose to my mind—I have prayed for each and all of you—you in these pews have been brought before God in prayer—I am nothing, a wreck, a voice, yet sent to speak. And again and again I have left the pulpit, which I entered jaded, as fresh as if I had been drinking in the iced air of the

Alps. God gives physical strength for spiritual exhaustion.

One closing word must be said. I implore my younger brethren to beware of throwing into parochial cares, often most secular, or even into the details which are needed for the production or performance of a "bright service," the time, strength, and fervour which are required for preaching. It is worse than folly to disparage this, the *magnum opus* of the Christian minister. It is to ignore the emphatic and reiterated injunctions of the Holy Ghost. It is to discredit the blessed and brilliant annals of the Divine society in Apostolic and sub-Apostolic times. It is to affect stone deafness to the voices of the great prophets in the East and in the West, in Jerusalem, in Antioch, in Constantinople, in Northern Africa, in Rome. Even now, when the wits of women are exhausted to add to the inanities of what is termed worship, we see in a hundred ways that preaching is still the greatest power which God hath charged men to use. I see this in and beyond the Church of England. And as I know more, I hope, about myself than I do about other people, I desire to assure those for whose interest I suppose these papers are published, that in Liverpool I had one of the ugliest fabrics that was ever devised; it had the three unpardonable enormities, a flat roof, galleries at each side, with the organ in the west gallery, and a three-decker. Our service was simple; our singing congregational, without even the aid of a surpliced choir. The neighbourhood was decaying, and many a time a railway-engine blew off steam during the service or during the sermon. Yet that church was crowded. It held 1400 persons, and I have seen 1800 in it. I may be pardoned for knowing more than any one else as to the cause of which that congregation was the effect. The cause, the sole, efficient, and adequate cause was Christ's gracious fulfilment of His promise. It was the moral magnetism of the uplifted Saviour. Moreover, the same cause is dominant in Norwich. The cathedral services—Holy Communion, morning prayer, and evensong—are solemnly, beautifully, reverently rendered. Nor would I diminish by a semiquaver the dignity of sacred song. Yet, the people are not, as they ought to be, at these services. But in the nave the worship is simple. The hymns touch all hearts, and are sung by all voices. The message is sometimes more than twice as long as that which is delivered at the ornate services. The congregation is three times if not four times greater. And so I find in Norwich, what four-and-twenty years I found in Liverpool, that crowds of souls will listen for thirty and even forty-five minutes to a message which speaks of sin, salvation, sanctity, and strength. "Preach the Word."

# III

By the VERY REV. F. W. FARRAR, D.D.,
*Dean of Canterbury.*

No one could feel less desire than myself to offer any advice about the preparation of sermons, or could make less pretence for any qualification for doing so. I simply do what the editor asks me—I say something about my own methods and views, if methods and views they can be called.

First, let me say that the office of a preacher seems to me so sacred and so awful in its responsibility that I can hardly imagine any good man who does not feel utterly humiliated by his own shortcomings, and by the glaring contrast between the lofty ideal which he should have and the poverty-stricken failure of the reality. My predecessor at Westminster, Canon Kingsley, used to say, with the slight stammer which often gave a charming emphasis to his sentences, "Whenever

I walk up the choir of Westminster Abbey to the pulpit I wish myself d-d-dead; and whenever I walk back I wish myself m-m-more dead." How well can I understand his feelings! To see those vast multitudes; to know that they have come in the desire to gain inspiration or instruction; to feel that even if they have come to scoff there are voices which *could* make them remain to pray; to dread lest any folly, any vanity, any ignorance, any uncharity of one's own should infect with alien influxes the pure river of the water of God; to tremble lest the hungry sheep should look up and not be fed; to desire

"To preach as one who ne'er could preach again,
And as a dying man to dying men;"—

and yet to be well aware how infinitely one falls short of that high purpose:—all this should be enough to humiliate any man to the dust. The only thought that can lift him out of the dust is the thought that "God can send forth His Seraphim with fire from off the altar to touch and hallow the lips of whom He will." It is solely on God's aid that the preacher must rely.

He who gave eloquence to the stammering tongue of Moses, and the "unclean lips" of Isaiah, can use the poorest of us as His instrument.

> "This is His will : He takes and He refuses,
> Finds Him ambassadors whom men deny,
> Wise men, nor mighty, for His saints He chooses,
> No, such as John, as Gideon, or I."

After making what a man might be inclined to regard as his best effort, if ever for a moment he should suffer himself to listen to the silly whispers of vanity, yet, if he be a true man, with a high conception of his duty, he will feel inclined to say with one of the most thoughtful preachers of this generation—F. W. Robertson : "Eloquence, rhetoric, impressive discourses, &c., &c., &c., soft gliding swallows, and noisy, impudent tom-tits, is the true worth of the first orator in the world."

If then I am compelled, for a moment, to speak of myself, it is with entire diffidence and extreme reluctance that I do so.

I.—I do not know whether any hearer has ever taken the trouble to speculate whether my sermons are quickly or slowly written ; whether they take a long time to compose or a short time. In point of fact they take a very short time. If I am left uninterrupted (which is very rarely the case) I seldom take more than three and a half hours to write a sermon. I do not at all recommend this swiftness to others. It is said that Melvill sometimes gave seven hours a day to his sermons; and the great French orators, who preached so seldom, and mainly at great Conferences twice or thrice a year, made their sermons a subject of immense elaboration. No pains can be too great if leisure be available, and if additional labour produces a better result. But a working clergyman rarely has much time to spare. He must give to his sermons such time as he can command, not as much as he could desire. And, further than this, it may often happen that more time spent on a sermon would not improve it. Written *currente calamo* under the influence of some dominant thought or deep emotion it may leap like a spark from an anvil, and further pains might only envelop it in the white ashes of euphuism and conventionality. Few sermons produced more powerful effect than those of Dr. Arnold, yet they were often written in a single hour between morning and afternoon service.

II.—How is one to choose a text?

Personally I seldom hunt for a text. Some thought or subject is in my mind, and presents itself spontaneously. Sometimes it is suggested by a single text, sometimes it is not. When I write on one dominant theme I often select the most appropriate text afterwards. But if by any chance when I have to write a sermon I have no special text or subject in my mind, I have only to look at the Epistle and Gospel, or the Lessons, or the Psalms of the day, and then the only difficulty can be which text of several to choose. The Bible, if we read it rightly, becomes like Aaron's pectoral "ardent with gems oracular," over whose graven letters—as in the Rabbinic legend about the Urim and Thummim—glides the mystic light of heaven, and spells the letters into ever new meanings and messages. And then, when we have found one subject for a sermon, a little meditation soon shows it to be so inexhaustible in depth and riches that out of a single sermon there often naturally grow three or four more which become necessary to complete the train of thought.

III.—But I may safely recommend the practice

of occasionally preaching courses of sermons on separate books, and also single sermons on each book of the Bible as a whole. The leaves of the tree may be beautiful, but the forest is greater. Each text may be like a flint, and though it look rough and brown on the outside, shows within, when broken by the hammer, a Drusic cavity filled with crystals of amethyst. Or a text may be like a wave of the sea flashing in the noontide; or like a single grain of sand upon the shore, which, for one instant, the sunbeam glorifies into an opal or an emerald:—but the Bible, and each separate book of the Bible, is like the mountain-side strewn with such flints, or like the mighty sea, or like the great sea-shore. Is it not strange that any educated man would instantly tell you the subject and outline of a play of Shakespeare, but that many a clergyman could tell you nothing —if suddenly asked—of the central idea and general plan of any particular Epistle of St. Paul?

IV.—But what should be the main object of preaching? I answer without hesitation the instruction, the elevation, the salvation of human souls. A sermon may embrace some detail of social life, or some fragment of doctrine, but it will be worse than useless if it does not tend to promote true religion, which, as Benjamin Whichcote so truly defined it, is nothing else but "a good mind and a good life." The end of all doctrine is conduct. Love is the fulfilling of the law. If we would enter into life it is before all things necessary that we keep the Commandments. Creed without character, orthodoxy without holiness, externalism without love to our brother, is a sounding brass and a tinkling cymbal. A sermon which does not send its hearers away with the desire to love God more and serve Him better, and to show that love and do that service by greater kindness and fairness and mercy, is but a wasted opportunity. Every true preacher must be what Noah was, what St. Peter and St. Paul and St. James were, what the Lord Christ Himself was—a preacher of righteousness.

V.—How far is it essential that a sermon should be original?

It is, of course, a base and a wrong thing for any man to pass off as his own the unacknowledged words and thoughts of others; but, on the other hand, not one man in a generation is absolutely original. It may be said of preachers as the Elizabethan dramatist said of poets—

> "One poet is another's plagiary,
> And he a third's, till they all end in Homer."

We must be ready to seize suggestions from all quarters—

> "From Art, from Nature, from the Schools,
>    Let random influences glance
>    Like light in many a shivered lance
> That breaks about the dappled pools.
>
> The lightest wave of thought shall lisp,
>    The fancy's tenderest eddy wreathe,
>    The slightest air of song shall breathe
> To make the sullen surface crisp."

One thing however is essential. We must make every thought we utter our own, by rethinking it; by passing it through the crucible of our own minds. Most certainly what we say will be like an autumn tree, twice dead, plucked up by the roots, unless we have honestly planted it in the soil of our own souls, from whatever source the seedling come.

VI.—Illustration is surely very desirable if it comes naturally and spontaneously from our own memory and the stores of our own reading. It is very rarely, I think, that preachers should eke out the poverty of their own thoughts by having recourse to books of anecdotes, illustrations, and such "loitering gear."

VII.—As for direct quotations from others, it is an immense temptation sometimes, not to our laziness but to our self-distrust, to quote—of course they must be frankly quoted as not our own—the words of others, who have expressed what we mean ten times more eloquently than we could have expressed it ourselves. But this should be done sparingly. A modern preacher got the nickname of "Elegant Extracts" because his sermons sometimes sounded like a mere string of selections. We should avoid that danger. Our own may be "a poor thing," and yet, if it be genuinely our own, the home-spun garb may sometimes be more effective for our use than the rich robes which others have worn, even though they be stiff with embroideries and gold.

VIII.—I am conscious of the defect of sometimes quoting too much poetry. My excuse is twofold. On the one hand, from boyhood upwards, when my memory was much more retentive than now it is, large stores of poetry accumulated themselves in my mind, though I never consciously learnt them by heart. They were among the choice treasures of my life, and sometimes force themselves into my words. And, on the other hand, I have always regarded, and still regard, the great poets as our deepest spiritual observers and our greatest moral teachers. It has ever been my own delight to be a humble learner at their feet while they sat "with their garlands and singing robes about them," and I may be sometimes tempted to believe that others may find, even in their most familiar words, the ever fresh delight which they have given me.

IX.—And now I have sufficiently worn my heart upon my sleeve for daws to peck at. I will only add that I regard nature, and art, and biography, and history, and literature, as great heaven-ordained teachers of mankind. They are books of God which, the more wisely and humbly we study them, become more and more fitted to explain and enforce and illustrate those messages of God which we read in Scripture, and those which He speaks to us, to every man each in the deep of his own heart. We can deliver no message if we have received none. To discriminate, to understand,

and to utter those truths which God has clearly manifested to ourselves, which He intends us to utter and to interpret to our brethren who are in the world; above all, to feel and to know, though it passes knowledge, the love of God in Christ; to feel and to know that God was in Christ, reconciling the world unto Himself, not imputing their trespasses unto them, and to make others partake of this personal conviction—that, I suppose, is the object of all sermons. Jesus is the Christ, the Son of God, and since it is only by believing on Him that we can have life through His name, it must be the preacher's highest and most constant aim to preach Christ—not in vain shibboleths, not in intricate dogmatic definitions, not by the mere wearisome iteration of "Lord, Lord," or any other formulæ—but to preach simple Christ to simple men, and to set forth "Him first, Him last, Him midst, and without end."

## IV

By the Venerable W. M. Sinclair, D.D.,
*Archdeacon of London.*

There can be no doubt whatever that a very large number of us do not take sufficient pains about exercising the enormous and incalculable privilege, that is allowed us by common consent, of weekly proclaiming the message of Christ.

There is no other subject in the world on which a whole assembly of people in every parish would come, every week at least, and listen in perfect silence for half-an-hour to the youngest neophyte.

The opportunity is absolutely unlimited and unparalleled. If adequately realized and earnestly used it might, under God, move the whole country. Its actual frequency and its occurrence as a matter of course, the very elements which ought to add to its extraordinary value in our eyes, and to make us daily fall down on our knees and thank God for this unobstructed opening for telling the people of

His unspeakable gift, tend in our unworthy hands to make us treat it with indifference, and to act as if we thought anything would do for the pulpit, either hurried essay without point or sympathy, or feeble measure of diluted commonplace, delivered on the spur of the moment, with endless repetitions and wearisome complement of "gag."

I do not mean that there are not probably more vigorous and sincere preachers in the Church of England to-day than there ever were before; but we are all aware that there are also too many to whom these descriptions apply. And there is reason why the whole of our clergy should not be free from such qualifications.

As one who has had the duty of asking questions of candidates for orders during the last eighteen years, I must express my amazement at the general absence of preparation on this, which, in the opinion of St. Paul, is equal in importance to any of their other duties. I except, of course, in a varying degree, those who come from the Theological Colleges, though in some of them, as far as I can make out, the training in preaching and reading is not very full. But the rest, as a rule, have none at all. Laymen would perhaps be prepared for this statement by what they too often hear in church; but Nonconformists would hardly believe it unless it was told them on good authority. There are young men who are actually pitched by scores and hundreds into the most sacred, important, and influential of all callings without any preparation whatever except the reading for the Bishop's examination. The attendance at two brief courses of Divinity lectures at the University, to which, however excellent, they are not obliged to pay attention, and on which they are not examined, can hardly count. They are expected, as soon as they are ordained, and with this entire absence of preparation, at an age when they are often not much more than boys in thought and habits, once a week to command the attention of congregations more or less educated, and to warn and instruct the people of God. Our present system is in many cases too much like this: "Get a well-meaning young man; examine and ordain him. Let him afterwards learn his duties as best he can."

Of course it may be said that what is needed is general information, especially theological, and the fire of living zeal in the heart. But what if there is little or no knowledge, and a very slender flame?

Under these circumstances it becomes of great importance to attract the attention of all candidates for orders and all young deacons and presbyters to the subject of preparation, and to convince them that though the Apostles, inspired by the teaching of our Lord, and with the full inspiration of the Holy Spirit, needed not to premeditate what they should say, because it would be given them in the very hour when they had to speak, yet with us, in these days of less direct inspiration, even if we were Whitefields, Wesleys, or Simeons, earnest and prayerful preparation is in all cases necessary.

It is easy and obvious to say all this, and yet not to be an example oneself of the ideal which one wishes to uphold. The writer is painfully conscious of his own deficiencies in the point of preaching as in other respects; but as it is part of the ancient duties of his office to be an "instructor of the clergy," he must not shrink from saying what seems to him the best, whether he can do it himself or not.

The difficulty which I have myself to contend with, and which I must constantly endeavour to overcome, is want of time. As a rule, I think of my subject on the Sunday before, turn it over in my mind during the week, collect on Saturday all the commentaries and books which will illustrate it, secure four or five consecutive hours on Saturday evening, and write the sermon straight off without pause or interruption. This does not give proper time for re-writing, reflection, alteration, excision, addition, or lightening. But my time, during every week of the year, except the autumn holidays, is more full of work than can be properly got through, and it is very difficult indeed to concentrate the mind and shut out other things except at such a special occasion.

The first point in preparation is to wrestle in prayer with God and ask Him Himself for a message. We believe that we have His Holy Spirit, that He will put into our minds good desires, and that we have only to give ourselves up more completely to His influence in order truly and really to be guided by Him. We must pray that we may be emptied of ourselves, that we may be stripped of all vanity, ambition, prejudice, prepossession, unfairness, unreasonableness, and anything else that may hinder the free operation of God's

Divine power in our minds and hearts. The desire to show off, to be thought clever, to be considered eloquent, to vie with some other preacher, all this is fatal to the delivery of a message from God. It is impossible to exaggerate the seriousness of the office, or to treat it with too great a sense of reality. There they are, the sheep of God's pasture, waiting to be fed. It may be the only food they will get during the whole week. There are you, the appointed one to feed them. Miserable trifler and traitor, what punishment is sufficient for you if you think of yourself in your method of feeding, or amble, mince, posture, and grimace in order to make the sheep think what a clever and beautiful shepherd you are, instead of going straight to the point of your duty as a serious man, and thinking only of giving them the very best and most wholesome food that you can provide? I wish every young clergyman could read "His Mother's Sermon" in Ian Maclaren's *By the Bonny Briar Bush*. The young preacher has come from his Scottish University to a remote country parish full of sublime metaphysics. He has prepared with exquisite care a discourse that ought for ever to crush some philosophical or theological heresy. He has been thinking of a University audience, and imagines that his powerful and eloquent thesis will be talked of far and wide over the country, and reach perhaps to the famous gates of the very College itself. And then he remembers the promise that he made to his mother, a true and humble Christian saint, that he would always preach Christ. There is a prolonged struggle. But at last the magnificent oration goes behind the fire, and in the rustic church next day, brought by his mother's love into full communion with the Holy Ghost, he pours out his soul to his people in simple earnest Evangelical fervour which pierces many a hard heart, and brings Christ Himself before the eyes of all in a way that consoles and satisfies and strengthens every hearer.

The next point is, the steady, consistent, watchful, sincere cultivation of our own Christian character. As we live, we shall preach. I do not mean to say that a preacher has not the right to set before himself as well as before his people an ideal which he has not yet himself been able to attain. But there must be the honest desire to attain it. If he goes beyond what has been at any rate sometimes his experience, and merely writes down what he thinks he ought to say, without any real participation in its true meaning, then there will be a false and hollow ring of insincerity in his utterances, which will be entirely ineffective, and will interest nobody. If, when you are preparing your message, there remains in your heart the memory of faults consciously indulged and unrepented, your sermon will be indeed a sorry farce. Away with such an impertinence from the light of the sun. Do not dare to speak in God's name if you feel yourself a hypocrite. Better that you should humbly read to the flock some wise and good man's words, than that they should be affronted and injured in God's house by the burlesque of an actor preaching what he does not believe, or dealing out to them warnings and exhortations when he knows that there is a lie in his right hand. Down on your knees, and with all your heart plead for God's grace of repentance, and ask for strength instantly to resolve effectually and unreservedly to put away the fault from you. Do not pretend that you, as an ordained minister of the Word, cannot need such self-abasement confession, and sorrow. Minister or not, God knows all about you, whether you admit your fault, or imperfection, or whatever it may be, or endeavour to conceal it from yourself and Him. You have St. Paul's own example to encourage you : " I therefore so run, not as uncertainly ; so fight I, not as one that beateth the air : but I keep under my body, and bring it into subjection : lest that by any means, when I have preached to others, I myself should be a castaway." We should be daily studying the Word of God, not as a mere mechanical duty, nor even only as material for our teaching, but to see whether we are really living ourselves in the very spirit of the Gospel.

However strongly we may be persuaded that we have received the fire of the living coal in answer to earnest, determined, and resolute prayer, we cannot suppose that we are relieved from the proper exercise of our own faculties. In receiving a message from God, it must necessarily be a selection from amongst resources within our own experiences and knowledge. So the choice of a subject comes next. We trust to be guided to a subject, and to be strengthened and disciplined in our treatment of it ; but we have to think what subjects are available. The best subject is the expository. We may either gather considerations in support of the truth of the principle contained in the text or paragraph we have taken, or we may deduce and apply the lessons which it contains, or both. But when we consider that the Bible contains the revelation of God's will for man and His salvation, the actual words of the Divine Saviour Himself, the inspired words of His Apostles and disciples, we can hardly deny that to bring these home to the hearts of our hearers in all their fulness and variety is the highest aim that we can have. It is this that gives the sermons of Dr. Vaughan their force and authority, and which, beyond all the charm of style, is the secret of the power of J. H. Newman's volumes. The long courses of directly expository sermons at Quebec Chapel by Magee, Alford, John Hampden Gurney, and Canon Francis Holland, had a lasting effect upon life in London. Other instances might be quoted. The thirty or forty volumes of Simeon's well-considered outlines, treating of almost every important passage in Holy Scripture, had an excellent effect on the preaching of his innumerable disciples, as different as can possibly be conceived from the lamentable and unworthy sneer that the Evangelicals preached solely from two chapters in the Epistle to the Romans. The congregation feel that their teacher is not preaching himself, but Christ Jesus the Lord, and that he is doing his best to explain to them the bearing of God's manifold truth on every circumstance and aspect of their lives. For this end it will be a great help to the preacher if at his own daily family prayers he carries out the old time-honoured habit of extempore exposition of Scripture after due preparation. With regard to the subject for Sunday, it should always be adopted and fixed, as I said, the Sunday before, and remain as a pivot in the mind during the ensuing days of the week, towards which the thoughts will naturally and instinctively flow. It is advisable to keep a book, or an envelope, and put down subjects as they occur to you. Something flashes across your mind, owing to some thought or incident, and if not committed to paper may easily be forgotten.

The systematic study of a commentary is a necessary preliminary and accompaniment to expository teaching from the Bible. It is deplorable how often ignorance is shown of this, the most important of all subjects, by candidates for Orders in the General Papers on the Old and New Testaments. Intimate knowledge of Holy Scripture for illustration and reference is clearly indispensable. Best of all is it when this is co-existent with life itself, and has been interwoven with all the developments of personal experience from the beginning. Whatever I possess in this way is largely owing to the most delightful and Christian of homes, the wisest, kindest, and best of parents, and to four happy years in the sixth form under one of the ablest, most discriminating, and most truly religious of Head Masters. But where these advantages have not been available, the defect can always be made up through the quiet and prayerful use of commentaries. Where resources permit it, the preacher will desire to gather round him the best of those who have written on different books—Alford, Ellicott, Lightfoot, and the others. The best and most helpful series as a whole I have found to be Lange's, in which you get the ripest results of orthodox German learning, as well as a summary of the interpretations of English and American scholars. It is hardly necessary to say that in the New Testament, at any rate, it is essential to read the passage in the original to see the proper force of the words.

The sermon must have a distinct unity and object. It is not a bad plan to write down the subject of the sermon in the Preacher's Book in the vestry after it has been delivered. If you do not yourself know what it has all been about, you cannot expect that knowledge from the congregation. The best rule is to state the general drift of the passage or the argument at the beginning, then to divide the subject under different heads which will cover the ground, and to end with a summary and exhortation. In this way your own thoughts will be clearer, and your hearers, having main points on which to hang what they have learnt, will be able to remember the rest.

It is necessary also at once to put yourself in sympathy with the people assembled. Speak to them directly. Show them that they have a personal interest in the subject that you are introducing. Find some common ground between yourself and them. Prove to them that you care for them, that they are not merely conventionally "brethren," but really and truly brothers and sisters in Christ Jesus, and that you have put yourself in their place, and can understand their wants and troubles. Speak without any reserve whatever, as the minister of God, forgetting for the time the accidents of your own life and position outside. Let them feel immediately that you are not stiffly, constrainedly, and self-consciously going through a performance, but that you have something to tell them, and that every word and idea has its own place and meaning, and is not put in merely to fill up. Let the message be real, and the manner affectionate and impressive as coming from your own heart.

In this connection it should of course be remembered that congregations greatly differ. Some are mainly fashionable, some mainly of high education, some commercial, some of artisans, some of the labouring class, some mixed. What would suit one of these in style, matter, and manner might not suit another. The establishment of the bond of sympathy in each case might be rather different. The pedantic academical essay, and the ill-hung, unpremeditated, loose, laboriously padded sentences would be equally unsuited to all.

Besides the study of Holy Scripture there must be a no less earnest study of life. You may understand the lessons of the Bible ever so well, but if you do not understand human nature your applications will be fired into the air. In your daily visits amongst your people you must be studying character in its infinite and inexhaustible varieties. You will get more help for your sermons from this than from any other study except that of the written revelation itself. You will find out what people are thinking, what puzzles them, what are their sorrows and weaknesses, how differently the same things affect different people, and those innumerable varieties of light and shade which make human beings so profoundly interesting. You will be able to come down from the abstract to the concrete, and the people will find something in your sermons that touches them, goes to their heart, appeals to the facts of their experience, is not like bubbles blown in the air, moves them, and remains with them as a reality. Your congregation will grow.

And parallel with this all young preachers should keep a common-place book for the insertion of illustrations, facts, thoughts, and ideas which come across them in their daily reading and experience. There are, of course, encyclopædias, dictionaries of quotation in prose and verse, the great Pulpit Commentary with its wonderful array of references, collections of anecdotes, and of notable and beautiful passages, and the like. But what you have gathered for yourself is far more real to you, and comes with fresher force to the hearers. It is in a secondary sense original, because although it is not your own creation, yet you have found it and made it your own. In history, ethics, poetry, science, in fact in all branches of reading, you will find illustrative matter. In the newspapers, in your every-day contact with human beings, if your mind has grown into the habit of observation, you will be quick to find things that will strengthen your teaching in the pulpit. You will remember how many of our Lord's lessons were conveyed in picturesque examples from daily life.

With regard to style, whether you are writing or going to deliver an oral address, it is well to read over a passage first from some powerful and eloquent writer, Macaulay, Froude, Newman, or Farrar, so as to get a good ring of vigorous English into the head. But it is a great mistake to imitate any one in particular. Young men insensibly get into a habit of this kind at different epochs, as one or another preacher becomes famous and popular. At one time it was Canon Liddon, and the young men fell into long sentences and melodious and highly-pointed intonation. At another time it might be Bishop King of Lincoln, and they would adopt an affectionate and easy tone of fatherly simplicity. But in Bishop King's sermons the real point is the genius; and in the young men the genius could not be expected to be present, and an empty affectation of extreme simplicity was the chief remainder.

Besides knowing something of the rules of composition, and the leading principles of addressing an audience, which come under the general head of "Rhetoric" without implying any effort at being "rhetorical," there is a great deal to be learnt in the management of the voice, and in the way of understanding how to produce variety in inflection suitable to different topics. There is nothing in this really artificial; it is simply finding out both by principles and practice how to catch the attention of the audience, and how insensibly to make the best of what you have to say. For perfection of delivery I should like to be permitted, without offence, to mention the late Archbishop Magee, Bishop Boyd Carpenter of Ripon, and Canon Fleming. Some men, of course, are born orators, and this gift comes to them by nature. But no nation can be expected to produce at one time 20,000 born orators; and most of us could make our sermons a great deal more interesting by a little knowledge and practice of this kind. I think I mentioned this point in a paper on "My First Sermon," contributed a short time ago to another series. I may be forgiven for saying that I had a great example in my father, who had a wonderfully rich voice, and a most varied, impressive, and finished delivery. But I did not in the least know how to attempt the same results, and was much vexed at my own monotony, until I went to the Professor at the Royal Academy, Mr. Walter Lacey. Nobody would accuse me of mentioning myself as an example in this respect; I only wish to say how much I privately feel that I owe to his lessons, and how sure I am that nearly all of us need certain points of this kind to be explained on setting out on our career of giving addresses weekly to all sorts and conditions of men.

Preparation will, of course, vary in some degree on the point whether the sermon is from a full manuscript, or from notes, or entirely oral. I have no doubt myself that oral delivery, with or without notes, is the most interesting and impressive to the great mass of the people. The answer to the question whether we should insist on adopting it for ourselves, depends on two points: whether we have a good memory, and whether we have sufficient confidence. There is no point on which people differ so greatly from each other as memory. My own, for example, is most deplorably defective, and no pains that I can take will improve it. Some people, on the other hand, are so strong in that respect that it is no trouble to them to learn a sermon by heart. Others can compose a sermon in their heads, and deliver it without even writing it down. Simeon, as is well known, found his delivery from manuscript duller than he wished, and he disciplined himself to preach with great power and eloquence from notes. In this matter each must judge for himself.

Of the message itself we are not asked in this series to speak. But however high, divine, and pure the message itself, it will be wise to bring it sometimes into relation with the concerns of human life. As theology treats of the Creator, it will be well to know something of the elements of modern science. As Christ's teaching is the highest system of ethics, we ought to know its bearing on the various human philosophies of morals. Practical questions will sometimes present themselves in which we can prove our sympathy with human aspirations and difficulties; questions about capital, competition, value, wages, the depreciation and enhancement of money, the rights of labour, sanitation, the dwellings of the poor, and the like; subjects to which we should not devote whole sermons, but which will naturally occur as illustrations when we show how the Christian spirit is the true atmosphere for improving the condition of mankind, temporal as well as spiritual. It is also greatly desirable that these subjects should be lifted from mere material aspects into the higher region of morality and religion. History cannot be neglected, especially that of our own country; examples of virtue and the reverse are most useful. Biographies of national heroes should be known for illustration; the ways of God in dealing with our people are surely matter for grateful record.

It is said of the lamented Bishop Thorold that in order to keep himself always in the homiletic spirit he read a sermon every day. The great models should certainly be studied: South, Barrow, Massillon, Bourdaloue, Bossuet, Fénélon, Lacordaire, Simeon, Chalmers, Guthrie, Caird, Arnold, Melvill, Newman, Robertson, Kingsley, Temple, Westcott, Lightfoot, Church, Liddon, Vaughan, Farrar, Boyd Carpenter, Magee, Talmage, Spurgeon, Thorold, and the like.

In conclusion, no labour can be too great for this most important part of our calling. Remember what St. Paul thought of it: "Christ sent me not to baptize, but to preach the Gospel." Think of the work bestowed on speaking by Demosthenes, Cicero, or Massillon. Think of Massillon producing works which men asked to hear again and again, like his *Carême*, and heard with delight. Avoid under-estimating the capacity of your people; even the uneducated have common-sense, and are shrewd and intelligent. What all alike want is clear and impressive information and instruction. It is your one great inestimable opportunity of bringing God before them, and showing them His greatness, goodness, and glory, and helping them to repent, and turn to Him, and work for Him and for His human family.

# V

## By the Rev. H. B. Tristram, D.D., F.R.S.,
### *Canon of Durham.*

The subject on which I am asked to write is one on which I have no right to speak with any authority; the more so, that so far from being a trained expert, there are, I suspect, very few men who have been so absolutely without training on this subject as myself. Whatever I have learned, has been acquired through a series of blundering failures; and I feel much in the position of an amateur in mechanics, who having never served his time should attempt to lecture the trained engineers, in some great workshop, on the mechanical powers. During a ministry of half-a-century, very few men have had so rarely until latterly an opportunity of hearing any other voice than their own in the pulpit.

Often have I envied the advantages enjoyed by the young curate of the present day, working under an experienced pastor of the flock. Anything like pastoral training, whether before or after ordination, was in my youth all but unknown. There were then no theological colleges excepting one or two "back doors," as they were called, for Durham and King's College were but in their infancy. Yet, though direct training for the pastorate ought surely to be a necessity, as much as for the medical or legal professions, I hope I may be pardoned for expressing the opinion, that the products of our modern theological colleges, Highbury excepted (of course I am not speaking of Halls, like those of Ridley and Wycliffe), do not stand out pre-eminently above those of their compeers, who have had merely a University education.

But to return to my own early experience, or rather inexperience. I had, at Oxford certainly, the opportunity of pulpit instruction. For four years in the morning I was generally taught by Manning, Newman, and Heurtley; in the evening I was regularly fed at St. Ebbe's, by the curates, Baring and Waldegrave. Immediately on taking my degree I went to Italy, taking with me *Richard Hooker, Pearson on the Creed, Jewel's Apology*, and

*Burnet on the Thirty-nine Articles*, which, with my Hebrew Bible and Greek Testament, constituted my theological library. *Bishop Butler* I had taken up for my degree. I remembered a saying of Bishop Phillpotts, "The man who with his Bible has mastered Butler, Hooker, Jewel, and Pearson, even if he have read nothing else, is no bad divine." I was ordained in the week of my twenty-third birthday, and at once entered on the curacy of an extensive Devonshire country parish of 2,000 souls, with a rector non-resident from ill health. From that day I had to preach generally three times a week. Would that I had had the firm will of the present Dean of Norwich, to give three hours to pulpit preparation before breakfast! Three days in the week were occupied in sick visiting in the widely-scattered parish, which could not have been accomplished without continual riding, and it was on horseback that I usually worked out my sermons; which may partly account for their jerky character. Two days were filled up with visiting the sick and aged in the large village, and with the schools, for in those days this was a part of his duty which no curate ever dreamt of shirking.

Saturday was supposed to be free, and on the first Sunday in the month I exchanged with some kindly neighbour in priest's orders, and so was relieved from one week of sermon preparation. What I should have done I know not, had it not been for the kindly advice of an old widow lady, the principal person in the parish, who called on me the day after my arrival and frankly said, " Now you will have no time to compose all your sermons. Do not try. Take my advice, and never attempt to compose more than one sermon a week, and let me suggest to you to copy your morning sermon from Heber or Hare, which I shall be glad to lend you, and make no secret of it." This advice I gratefully followed.

My method of preparation from the first was that, I suppose, adopted by all my brethren. On the Sunday evening (for afternoon, not evening, services were the popular ones in those days) I carefully selected my text, and generally contrived to have the skeleton or heads on a scrap of paper before I retired to bed. I do not know why it is, but I have always found that work begun before retiring to rest is much better carried on than if begun in the morning. On looking back, and thinking of the temptations that have since beset me in preaching, I have always felt thankful that in my first and only curacy I was conscious of no critics, my congregation, though very large, being, with the exception of one family, entirely agricultural and artisan, to whom, though so young, I was not afraid of speaking plainly and simply.

Very different was my next sphere. Shortly after being ordained priest I was compelled, being broken down in health, to seek a warmer climate. And here I may remark on the practical common-sense shown by Bishop Phillpotts in examination for Orders. The examination for the diaconate was certainly what, even now-a-days, would be called stiff; not only translations from Augustine into English, but of St. Chrysostom into Latin, and searching questions on the English Reformation in an honest, Protestant sense. But this once passed, the Bishop troubled us no more with the learning of the schools. It was men, not books, that was the testing-point of the examinations for priest's orders—such questions as "Called upon to visit a sick person who was under strong conviction of sin, or one utterly indifferent, or one wholly ignorant, or one under morbid depression, what passages of Scripture would you select, and how would you apply them to each case?" There were similar questions on the catechizing of children, and the like.

In my next three years, on the other side of the Atlantic, I found myself the one clergyman in a little island of the group where I was acting naval and military Chaplain, with the spiritual care of a hospital of 120 beds, for soldiers and man-of-war's men. I had two distinct congregations, the one military, the other naval and dockyard. Here I felt for the first time how truly the "fear of man" is "a snare," a sort of self-consciousness continually leading one to think, especially at the military service, how the officers would take my address, instead of simply seeking to deliver Christ's message without regard to man. But I was soon taught a lesson. Any one who knows the British Army knows that in almost every regiment there are to be found outspoken, godly men. The Colonel of the regiment and the Commanding Engineer were two of these. They did not hesitate to take the young Chaplain by the hand, and one of them in particular—the late Sir William Gordon, R.E., with whom I had the privilege of sharing quarters for a year,—would talk over with me my sermons, both before and after delivery, pointing out to me how to speak to men as men, on a common platform, of a common Saviour.

Amongst my other duties was the daily visit to the hospital for an hour and a half, always entering in the register-book in the hall the exact time of my entrance and departure. I think that here was my true education for the ministry. The ten minutes' exposition to convalescents, for which previous preparation was needful, was a useful training for preaching without book. Thinking over the special cases that I had visited the day before, my first work after breakfast was to find some passage specially adapted to one or two of them, and then to endeavour to frame comments that should come home without seeming to others as personal.

Returning to England, my next sphere for eleven years, though often interrupted by absence on account of health, was a small country parish, under a model squire and his wife. He was far my senior in years, a brilliant Oxford scholar, and a well-read theologian. This was not, for me, a school for extempore preaching, but for careful well-digested composition, with sensitive reference to a higher tone of criticism, and not unsuited to a congregation largely composed of well-educated, hard-headed Scotchmen, free to remark, the next time of meeting, on both doctrine and illustration. The kindly hints I received from my Squire were of no little value. He used to impress upon me the importance of never isolating a text, but of always treating it as part of a whole, especially if taken from the Epistles, or, as his border-steward also quaintly expressed it to me, "I like to hear a man that looks at the Romans or the Hebrews 'end on.'"

It was here that I made my first essay in open-air preaching. There was a large colliery in the parish, though the colliers all lived outside it. I felt it my duty to do something for my neighbours, and accordingly announced my intention of preaching on the pit-heap after "pay." It happened to be when the wonderful comet of 1858 was just overhead. With inward tremor, for the Church was in no good odour there, I mounted the "heap" opposite the colliery office, and took the comet for my text. There was a goodly crowd around me, who gave me an attentive hearing until, on my reminding them that "we have to do with a God who hears and answers prayer," a well-known leader among the men cried out, "Aye, there's one good prayer in the Bible, 'Avenge me of mine adversary.' Down with the capitalists." I do not know how, but the inspiration seemed to seize me, and at once I replied, "That prayer is not for him. My friend should have read a few verses further on, and he would have found the prayer for him, 'God be merciful to me a sinner.'" A woman in the crowd called out, "Ah, Jock, the priest has given thee one in the mouth now." Jock slunk away, and from that day I *had* those men.

At the conclusion of that service the primitive local preacher came up to me patronizingly and said, "Weel, sir, you're all very well 'to bank,' but ye cannot work the lower seam like us."

On removing to my next charge, another country parish but much larger, I determined to attempt preaching without book at the evening service, remembering the advice of Robinson, of Leicester —" No man should preach extempore till he has preached from book for fourteen years, and even

## ON SERMON PREPARATION 91

then for fourteen years more he will never have preached without finding that he has forgotten something he ought to have said, and said something he ought not to have said." And he was right. Here I remained till my removal to Durham, where, I need not say, I, for one, do not feel competent to address a University congregation of graduates and undergraduates, with, perhaps, a dozen first-class men and Senior Wranglers among them, without very careful preparation and the weighing of every word. Elsewhere, I am more free. As the master of one of our great schools once remarked to me after I had addressed the boys, "You preached as if you were not in Durham Cathedral to-day; you preached as if you knew you had no cynics before you."

But enough of self. May I add a few words on the preparation and delivery of sermons in general, and of missionary sermons in particular? As I am not here preaching a sermon I need say nothing of the first need of preparation, communion with God, and that no word can be spoken with profit for God, to God's people, which does not come from God, by the guidance of God's

Spirit sought by communion with Him. But even thus we have this treasure in earthen vessels, and the flavour of the wine may depend much on the vessel into which it is put. If that vessel be not clean, it will discolour the liquor; if it be tainted by the poison of false doctrine, it will render it unwholesome. And, even in more trifling matters, to continue the simile, if it be poured out hastily or carelessly, much may be lost; if poured out aimlessly, it may miss the soul for which it was intended.

Considered thus, there is much in the accessories of preaching, in delivery, in manner, in intonation. I remember hearing Mr. Moody, in one of his addresses *ad clerum*, advise us, if I understood him rightly, to select our subject, arrange our heads, and then seek for a text to fit it. This is not my plan. I would choose the text first, but carefully noting its context, without which the preacher may easily be led into wresting Scripture, as in the well-known instance of "Hear the Church," or, as I have heard in our own cathedral, "We have an altar." I do not mean to say, choose the text apart from the subject; but take, for instance, the subject to which the services of the day point, and then consider from what passage of Scripture we can best draw the lessons.

This by no means excludes the selection of a typical or illustrative text, or even of a text as a motto, when not distorted. The preacher was warranted, during the Indian Mutiny, in taking for his text "Behold the voice of the cry of the daughter of My people, because of them that dwell in a far country"; or, in preaching a missionary sermon, to take the command "Make this valley full of ditches," as illustrating the need of man's work as well as of the Holy Spirit's fructifying power. When the text has been chosen, let us remember that every sentence of the Word of God is like a gem with many facets, which can be looked upon on every side, and turned every way. One of the most effective preachers I ever knew, to an entirely working-man congregation, and one in which men largely predominated, never had but one idea in each sermon. He was a man without either learning or eloquence, but he took his text, and turned it every way, and illustrated it from every quarter till it was impossible for the simplest hearer not to carry away that idea. This is the secret of his success.

Again, how much there is in manner. I do not mean an affected earnestness, which is very soon detected, but an unconventional earnestness. I have often heard men speak on a platform of whom I have thought at once, Why can he not speak in the pulpit as he does here? Conventionalism of manner is as besetting a fault as conventional phraseology. We remember the reply of a great actor to a great preacher, who asked him, "How is it that you can stir the emotions of crowds by the utterance of what they and you know to be fictions, while I, uttering what they and I know to be truths, cannot stir them at all?" "Because," he replied, "you utter truths as if they were fictions; I utter fictions as though they were truths." It is largely thus, through formalism and want of earnestness of manner, that, in many quarters, preaching has sunk into disrepute. What heart could possibly be reached by such a performance as I once heard in a continental chapel, where the youthful preacher, or rather priest, as he would have called himself, after reading the first lesson, Deborah's Song, in a monotone, intended to be musical, read a sermonette of ten minutes, in the same monotone, without once lifting his eyes or moving a muscle? He believed he was imitating Newman.

Not less important than delivery is the choice of good illustrations. To the uneducated, nothing rivets the teaching like an apt illustration. But here let the preacher beware and be sure that he knows the technicalities of his subject. A celebrated Mission-preacher the other day unfortunately utterly destroyed the effect of his address to the gardeners and others who were present by informing them that the good fruit-tree was obtained by grafting a wild branch on to a good stem! When a dockyard Chaplain, I once secured the aid of an eloquent American bishop, whose sermon certainly riveted me. The next day, meeting the boatswain of the yard, who was a great critic, I remarked to him, "That was a grand sermon, Mr. S——, that we heard yesterday." "Well, I don't know, sir," he replied, in the same deep roar which he had used when he was Lord Nelson's boatswain's mate, "I only hope he knows his own business better than he knows mine." "Why, what was the matter?" exclaimed I. "Why, didn't you hear? He talked about sails hanging idly from the mast, as if any landlubber ever saw a sail hanging from anything but a yard yet!" That one slip had spoiled the impression of a noble sermon. Thirty years after I met Bishop Bedell again in England, and told him the story. He said, "I well remember that sermon; would that I had known the criticism years ago, the lesson would have been invaluable."

Next let us beware of the slipshod mixed metaphor in which I have more than once heard young preachers indulge. This may culminate in such figures as in Church Defence, "Let us stick to the old ship, for she is on the rock!" and "The spark is already kindled, let us water it," "A noble cedar in the Lord's vineyard." Another danger is the too frequent use of conventional phraseology, especially on doctrinal topics. In the north of England, many members of our congregations, having been trained on Presbyterian lines, and without much real grasp of the subject, are very apt to test a preacher's orthodoxy by his use of familiar theological catch-words, and this proves a snare to superficial preachers. I remember a young man of much fluency but with a somewhat slender grasp of the Evangelical truths which he intended to hold, complaining to his rector that he found himself always preaching practically the same sermon, though he changed his text. His rector quietly replied, "Do you ever read?" and was answered, "I have no time for reading." "That accounts for it," was the reply.

With regard to the length of a sermon, I have often found a terrible temptation to what may be called preaching against time, *i.e.* filling up with padding when one's ideas are exhausted. I do not believe that it is profitable to lay down, either for one's self or others, any fixed rule as to the length of sermons. Congregations in the north, especially the uneducated, are not only more patient of long sermons than southern and town congregations, but even demand them. I had once taken for my text, "Pray without ceasing." A Scotch parishioner and communicant remarked to me afterwards—"That was a grand sermon you gave us, but if my old minister at Kelso had had the handling of it he would have made an hour out of it."

On the contrary, a well-known Bishop of the early part of this century rebuked his curate (a relative of mine) thus: "You preach too long, Mr. H——. St. Paul fell into the same error, and

Eutychus was killed." Hortatory addresses and doctrinal sermons, I have always found, should be short, but narrative or expository sermons, and especially missionary ones, where the preacher is familiar with the details of missionary work, may well extend to forty minutes or more without trying the patience of the congregation. But a preacher with a little experience will soon be conscious whether his hearers are tired or not. There is in congregations, as in other assemblies, an electric sympathy, negative as well as positive, and a pulse that can be felt.

When speaking of extempore sermons I do not mean *memoriter*. To learn a sermon by heart, as was the unfortunate fate of the Scotch ministers of the last century, would ever have been to me an impossible task; and by an extempore sermon I do not mean one without notes, for that is pretty certain to degenerate into the slipshod rhetoric easily acquired by any one of natural fluency. I mean a sermon which has been carefully thought out through the week; for, while making no pretence to the systematic preparation of the Dean of Norwich, my plan has been, the subject and text having been chosen, that it should be an uppermost topic of thought during the week, and any idea or illustration that presented itself meanwhile was jotted down on a scrap of paper on the study desk. Then, towards the end of the week, these thoughts and hints were reviewed, and mentally sorted out and a skeleton framed. I have generally found that one side of a half-sheet of note-paper to slip into my Bible was sufficient for this; the topics being clearly marked by numerals, so as to catch the eye at a glance; and one or two words will then suffice for each subject, illustration, or Scriptural reference.

If I may add from my own experience, I feel it dangerous to get up the exact words, for then, instead of preaching, I find my mind reverting to memory, and while uttering one paragraph I should be thinking of the next. If the preacher really knows his matter, the right words will present themselves at the moment. Beyond sometimes writing down a short peroration, I am not conscious that I have ever for either speech or extempore sermon set down the exact words I should use. Perhaps to do this requires some years' experience, and therefore it is well not to begin too early. Here comes in the apothegm of Lord Bacon, "Much reading maketh a full man, much writing an exact man, much speaking a ready man." This is the true order. First study, then apply and test the results exactly, then we may give them forth with profit to others.

I know I am expected to say a word on the missionary sermon, in which I have had some little experience. The missionary address is not generically distinct; yet, perchance, it may claim specific differentiation. I should say, in the first place, beware of taking too low a standpoint in setting forth missionary claims. Many men preach a missionary sermon in the same tone, and on the same lines, on which they would plead for a friendly society or other temporal charity. The claims of Missions stand on higher ground. "I have been asked," said a clergyman, "to come and plead for Missions. Plead for Missions! I should scorn to do so. Does the Queen, when she makes a proclamation, send forth her heralds to plead with the people for its observance? Rather do not her Commissioners of Assize declare the law, and say that it must be obeyed? And Christ's proclamation is the order, 'Go ye into all the world.'" Let us lay this down first, and take care that it is seen at once, that we look on the missionary's work not as one duty amongst many, but as the charter, on the fulfilment of the terms of which the existence of the Church depends. Let the one unbroken thread of a missionary sermon be, not missionary facts, but a missionary principle, with facts in illustration of that principle. For instance, I would not begin by depicting the misery of the heathen, and appealing to our Christian sympathy with them in their lost condition. Let us start from a higher platform, and point out that it is the love of Christ that must constrain His people in the first instance, and not merely even the love of souls. This is the first and great command of missionary law, and the second is like unto it. I think it is important for the edification of the hearers that whatever missionary facts or illustrations we employ should have a direct and evident connection with the doctrinal or spiritual lesson which I would educe from my text. If the text were "Ethiopia shall soon stretch out her hands unto God," let us take care that our missionary facts are from Africa and not from New Zealand, and, before preparing, take care that our sermon be not merely general. Diagnose the congregation. The Cathedral sermon will not do for the pit village.

A very different style of address is needed for University students—from amongst whom you may hope that volunteers may be drawn in answer to your prayers—from that which will arouse the sluggish faculties of a country congregation. In addressing the former, for instance, or in fact any educated congregation, few topics can be more profitable than to point out the contrast between, *e.g.* Buddhism and Christianity, and to show where the cold moon "Light of Asia" pales before the warm life-giving Sun of Righteousness. On one occasion I had been taking this topic in a southern Cathedral, the Bishop remarked to me after service, "You spoke of Buddhism. Do you remember Milman's definition of it? 'The vastest and fairest nothing that was ever passed upon mankind.'" I took the hint. It was supplemented shortly after by a suggestion from the Dean of another Cathedral, "You gave us Milman's definition of Buddhism, but you omitted Whittier's contrast—

> 'Nothing before, nothing behind,
>   The steps of faith
> Fall on the seeming void, and find
>   The rock beneath.'"

Missionary interest is, now-a-days, so generally diffused, that there are not many places which have not some connection, more or less close, with some special mission or missionary. It always tells, to draw our illustrations from such a mission. Then we should always avoid the abstract when we can use the concrete; never rest in generals when we can have particulars. Avoid statistics, except incidentally. The incidents of one conversion, briefly told, will lay hold of a congregation with far more power than a whole page of generalities.

But no man should attempt a missionary sermon without knowing something of missionary work. The literature of missions is now a library in itself. It is hard enough for the expert, impossible for the hard-worked pastor, to keep fully abreast of it, but any man can master the history and details of some one mission. I would suggest to my stay-at-home brethren, that if they thus follow Christ's work in some one field, even if it be not one of the most romantic, they will not find it difficult to preach an instructive and profitable missionary sermon.

In these desultory and, I fear, far too egotistic

remarks, I have taken for granted, that which must lie at the root of all effective preaching—that which is within the preacher himself, the preparation of heart. This has been effectively dwelt upon by others.

# VI

By the REV. H. C. G. MOULE, D.D.,
*Principal of Ridley Hall, Cambridge.*

THE largeness of the theme suggests of itself some limitations in the treatment. I propose to understand by "sermons" the sermons which a parochial clergyman has to prepare in the ordinary course of his ministry. Every clergyman has his exceptional calls and occasions, when either he addresses another pastor's flock, or has to address his own under especial circumstances; and such occasions may be, and when rightly met will be, times of inestimable opportunity, to be prepared for and used with all possible care and prayer. But we will not think of them now; our attention shall be given to the average and the rule.

As we approach this subject, however, let us first, in a way quite general, recall some obvious principles affecting all true preparation for the delivery of a sermon. And first, the necessity and sacred duty of *some* preparation, and the dangerous mistake of letting the intended sermon "take care of itself," perhaps with the thought that this is faith, and that the Lord will take care of it for us. Faith is never commended to us in God's Word as a substitute for diligence; it is rather to be a condition and stimulus to a diligence full of freedom, but also of purpose and of care. "Take no thought beforehand what ye shall say" is a precept not for the teaching pastor, but for the martyr before his unjust judges. "Practise these things (ταῦτα μελέτα)" is the message (1 Tim. iv. 15) of the Spirit by the Apostle to the man who has to shepherd and feed the flock. As a fact, slight and hurried preparation for a sermon leads only too directly to confusion of thought and statement, to a needless and tiring diffuseness, and so to languid and disappointed listening, and to quick oblivion. "I often do not know what my text will be five minutes before I mount the pulpit," said a fluent young preacher in the hearing of the late Bishop Daly, of Cashel. "Then I will undertake to tell you, young man," said the Bishop, turning round to him, "that the people don't know what the sermon has been about five minutes after you have come down."

Then, to linger a little still over more general thoughts on the matter, and to look at the outer rather than the inner aspects of preparation at present, we will remember that the work will always naturally divide itself between preparation of material and preparation of expression. As to the former, it is impossible, of course, to prescribe any process of routine. Not only must different men collect their material in different ways; the same man, unless his mind works with extraordinary and not quite enviable regularity, will go to work in different ways at different times. On one text, for instance, he will rightly take care to consult expositors, to verify and arrange quotations, to summon illustrations from all quarters. On another he will find his whole equipment in the Word itself, seen in the light which the Spirit has poured upon it through his own experiences of life and grace. All that we can say on this matter, in general and *à priori*, is that it is all important that genuine material should be somehow collected, and that the collection should be such as to be, under God, the man's own doing. We must prepare so that our brief allotted time in the pulpit shall be really filled with a solid supply of truth and thought, not with trite and ineffective utterances, which make no lodgment in either heart or mind. And that supply must be not a mere anthology of other men's sayings. Whatever be the source of this or that element in the message, it must have really passed through the preacher's own reason and soul, so as to be "truth through personality." Again, in most cases certainly, the collection of materials, while manifold from one point of view, should be single and simple from another. The sermon may speak of many things, but it will group them all round one thing as the ruling theme, or at most round a very few things, and those few things related to one another. The collection must have order, and the order must be determined by a purpose, by a recognized *message* which the man has heard and must deliver. No small part of true sermon preparation lies always in this direction; in the recognition of the "burthen," the message of the text, and in the consideration of the order and proportion which will best bring home that message. Here, again, it is impossible to lay down a routine. All that can be said is that some definite divisions will be almost always vital to effective presentation; divisions usually (not always) stated to the congregation, but always at least present to the preacher's own mind.

Then we come to the verbal expression of the material, and preparation for it. The whole question between written and unwritten sermons here arises; but I must perforce dismiss it with the remark that while very few men, so I think, can wisely dispense with writing in the early days of their ministry, and while some do well to write and to read their sermons to the last, the ideal for most congregations surely is the thoroughly prepared sermon, spoken not from a manuscript but —as to the diction of it—from the trustworthy instincts of the earnest and educated mind. In Canon Carus's *Memoir of Bishop M'Ilvaine of Ohio* (an admirable book, full of suggestion,) this is strikingly illustrated. In M'Ilvaine's early days as a preacher, at Washington, one of his hearers was the British Minister, Sir Stratford Canning, afterwards Lord Stratford de Redcliffe. With the oratorical instinct of a Canning he saw that the gifted young clergyman was hampered by the attempt to prepare beforehand the diction of his sermon, and then to recite it without manuscript. He called on M'Ilvaine, and advised him as a friend to prepare his matter more carefully than ever, but to leave his diction entirely to the moment; and the advice was taken with the best results. It is obvious that such counsel is appropriate only where the man is taking good general care to honour the Queen's English,—a care not always taken by us preachers. To leave to the spur of the moment the verbal expression of a particular sermon assumes that the ·man who has for a main part of his life-work the most sacred sort of public speaking is habitually careful to phrase his thoughts correctly in the common intercourse of life. The preacher will remember his pulpit, in this sense as well as in many others, wherever he is. He will be daily forming the habit of pure and true expression, by carrying that recollection with him. He will quietly train himself, not into a pedant whose vocabulary and grammar suggest the conversation-book, but into the worthy speaker of the noblest of living languages, English undefiled. Then when he stands in the pulpit with the message of his Lord he will speak with just the same freedom and just the same care as usual, making not the slightest change into a supposed sermon-dialect, but recollecting fully the holy gravity of the theme and the hour.

If one word more may be said on the subject of verbal expression, it shall be that if any phrase of a sermon may be meditated beforehand with some exactness, it is the first phrase, and the last. It is curious to observe how greatly any public address gains or loses in the way of securing attention and of leaving impression, by the presence or the lack of point and force in its opening and its close. And as to the close, let it by all means be so adjusted as to leave not *any* strong impression behind it but *the* strong impression which the preacher desires, under his Master's blessing, to be left by that particular sermon.

We return now to thoughts on the preparation particularly of the ordinary parochial sermon, the discourse of the Sunday morning, afternoon, or evening, or of the week-day service. I assume that my reader is no friend to that evil innovation, the sermon without a text. His first care is the choice of a text, longer or shorter, from that

"Word of God which liveth and abideth for ever," and which we at our ordination are specially enjoined to expound. Here again much offers to be said in detail; but I will only say in passing that most of us will do wisely to avoid, for our ordinary preaching purposes, texts which involve special difficulties in preliminary exposition; texts where great changes of rendering as compared with the Authorized Version are necessary, or are thought to be so; texts so very short that they almost forbid the division of the subject; texts so long that a concentrated message from them is almost impossible. This latter class of texts is often admirable for consecutive treatment in a course, but rarely for a single sermon. Then again, as Henry Venn the elder long ago remarked, it is well to incline to texts which by the marked solemnity or by the greatness otherwise of their own wording, will arrest at once the reverent attention of thoughtful hearers; Venn instances his own use of the text (Exod. xxxiv. 5), "The Lord descended in the cloud, and proclaimed the name of the Lord."

But what I would rather urge here, as to this part of sermon preparation, is that we should take pains to avoid a mere haphazard choice of texts, or what looks like it. It seems to me, I confess, a mistake when Sunday after Sunday, in the course of a settled parochial ministry, the "pastor and teacher" (Eph. iv. 11) reads to his people a text for which there appears no special reason, which bears no relation to the texts of other sermons, and the message from which is given as an isolated thing. Surely we should do what we can to give our stated ministry of teaching some wholeness and continuity—not for a moment as if such a purpose were to become a bondage, but it will surely be useful as a "guide and not a chain." With this end it may be well frequently to look for our text within the large limits of the Scriptures which will be read at the service in question; or to seek it as suggested by some truth made prominent in the Collect for the week; or, again, a course of sermons, shorter or longer, may be arranged and announced, on some connected series of foundation Gospel truths (there is abundant need for this at present); or on leading points of Christian duty or consistency; or by way of connected expositions on some important Scripture, some paragraph, chapter, or book. In this sort of work, which experience encourages me to think is not only extremely useful but often decidedly welcome and attractive to congregations, care will be taken to choose a portion which brings up a variety and succession of great truths, grouped round the one eternal theme, the Son of God; so that the course shall in some degree train or stimulate the hearers to connected and comprehensive views of the Gospel and of the Lord. What we preachers want is, on the one hand, never to wander away from "Jesus Christ and Him crucified"—alas for us and our people if we do; on the other hand, never to be really monotonous on the one glorious theme. We want to *walk round* " the wondrous Cross," as it were, and to see, with an insight ever new, all it has to reveal: to the sinner in his sleep; to the sinner awakened; to the sinner believing; to the believer working, suffering, living, dying; to the Church; to the world. Our message is one, and the longer we live, if we live indeed, the more we shall feel that we have no time in the pulpit for anything but Christ. But our message is infinite in its oneness; and we shall feel this also more and more as life goes on, if we so live that the Lord is much to us. And assuredly, if we pastors converse much with others, we shall realize more and more how urgently for their sakes we need to remember alike the manifoldness and the oneness of the message; all our blessings hid in Christ, all our life claimed by Christ, and He meanwhile "the same yesterday, and to-day, and for ever."

These last reflections lead me at once, for the remainder of my space, to a part of my subject which has all along been on my heart. I have just spoken of the preparation which lies in the thoughtful choice of text. How to proceed after that choice, as to collection and arrangement of materials, and assimilation of them, and as to verbal expression of the message; on these points I have touched, however passingly, in the earlier paragraphs. Now let me turn to that most vital of all parts of sermon preparation, the preparation of the man.

There is one profound difference between that sort of public speaking which we call preaching and many other sorts, I mean that alike the subject-matter and the commission of the preacher make it absolutely impossible to dissociate "the man and his communication." The preacher by his very office presents himself as a man directly, intensely, vitally concerned with his message. His message is Jesus Christ. And he stands in that pulpit, not because he has been hired to lecture, but because he has, at his ordination, assured the Church of Christ that her Lord has inwardly moved him to seek the "pastor-teacher's" work. More simply still, the message he delivers has infinitely grave and sacred bearings on every man who hears it; and he is a man, and he is listening to his own words.

So in order to the preparation of the sermon there is the utmost possible need that there should be preparation of the man. This preparation must, of course, be special and particular, in part; "mind, and soul, and heart, and will," must be made ready, in the Lord, for just *that* sermon, for its theme, its message, and its hearers. The man must set himself consciously to win the Master's presence and power for that individual action in His name, seeking to choose the text, and prepare the materials, and throw the whole into order, and bring the whole to bear upon the living souls whom he is to address, in the spirit of one who knows Who alone can grant supernatural results.

## ON SERMON PREPARATION

But behind all this particular preparation there must be going on what is of even greater importance, if possible—the preparation which is general, and runs all through life. If the sermon is to be prepared indeed, it must be a living action springing from a life which is preparing itself every day.

To give definiteness to the thought, let me divide it. The prepared sermon must be the outcome of a life which, in some various distinct respects, is always getting ready for the Lord's use. What are some of these respects?

I.—The man must know, and be growing in knowledge of, his Lord and Master. To me it seems that an incalculable difference between sermon and sermon often lies just here: that the sermons may be equally good otherwise, but that one of them somehow gives the impression that the man speaks at first hand of God in Christ, and the other suggests a secondary sort of knowledge. Alas for the ministry and for the minister, where this latter suspicion is true. Where it is so indeed, where the preacher "has heard of Him with the hearing of the ear, but his eye hath" not yet "seen Him," let the need be faced indeed, and let "sermon preparation" take for the while one supreme direction, that of seeking the Lord while He may be found, till He is found indeed. And then let it be seen to that a watchful intercourse with Him is maintained, in confession, prayer, praise, and obedience. So will our knowledge of Him grow; otherwise it will certainly decline. And a declining knowledge of Him will almost inevitably show itself in a declining power to speak for Him, whether in the pulpit or out of it.

If we would prepare to preach, we must prepare to pray. We must speak often and with adoring freedom to the Father, through the Son, in the Spirit, if we would speak for God to man. There must be a divine friendship, a friendship kept up "through all the changing scenes of life," so that the experience of what the Lord is and can be to His servant, shall be always enriched and increased with time. Such "growth in the grace and in the knowledge of our Lord and Saviour" (2 Pet. iii. 18) will be a perpetual preparation for the sermon work of His servant. It will give a holy freshness, versatility, and adaptability to the message about Him which otherwise cannot possibly be secured, no, not by the ablest and most thorough secondary preparations.

II.—The man must know, and be growing in the knowledge of, himself. I put this point second, for this among other reasons, that while some self-knowledge seems indispensable to our first coming to Christ, the deepest and most fruitful comes as the result of actual intercourse with Him. It is the *contact* that shows most profoundly, while most tenderly, the *contrast;* my darkness seen against His light, my weakness against His strength, my sin against His holiness, my folly against His wisdom. It is mysterious but it is true that where there really is the contact of true faith and surrender, in the grace of the Holy Ghost who joins us to the Lord, there, just there, will and do concur the two contrasted results—a blessed deliverance from sin's tyranny, and an intense and tender sense of sin—of our sin —in its vileness and condemnableness. And along with this side of self-knowledge is sure to be developed many another also; not the morbid self-scrutiny which weakens, but many and varied experiences of what life really means to the living soul in its realities of temptation, trial, duty, and service. All this will be a perpetual preparation for the sermon. It will show us in a thousand ways how, through our own hearts and lives, to see into others, so as to sympathize, to understand, to warm, to cheer, and to give just that sort of witness to Christ which shall adjust itself to real and not imaginary needs.

III.—The man must know, and be growing in the knowledge of, the flock of Christ committed to his care. This part of our "general preparation" links itself naturally to the two former. It cannot possibly be a substitute for them. But it is profoundly necessary as combined with them, in view of the sermon. It is one of the great duties of the "pastor and teacher" to remember the pulpit not only in his study, but in his round of visiting, and in the whole of his pastoral intercourse, even in those parts of it which may seem least directly sacred. For his Lord's sake he must keep his eyes, his ears, his heart open to all that thus passes before him, to all which thus unfolds the realities of life and character to him; he must do this not only for general reasons, but because of his sermons. The effect upon the sermons will be not that the solemn and blessed message, one and eternal, will be distorted into something narrow and local, but that it will be directed into the receptacle, however narrow, into which he longs to convey it, instead of being poured wastefully upon the earth. The man will not preach another Gospel. He will not make the Gospel parochial any more than he will make it the partisan of a political party or a social class. But he will, under God, bring the Gospel really to the parish, which is another thing. He will ponder his sermon, and he will preach it, with a preparedness which will result in many a heart's conviction that the Lord not only " tells us all that ever we did," but understands all that we have to do.

IV.—The man must know, and be growing in the knowledge of, his Bible. I place this last, not as being least, but that it may go with all our other remembrances as to preparation of the man. For indeed it is a *sine quâ non* in connection with them all. I do not attempt to say much about it; but I think most of my readers will agree with me when I urge its unmistakable necessity, and affirm that that necessity was never greater than now. To an astonishing degree lowered views of the Divine truth and authority of the Written Word have invaded the Church, within these five-and-thirty years, but above all within these last five or six. One result of those views, so far as they prevail, is quite inevitable; there will be an enfeebled study of the Bible in the sense in which the Lord bade us study it, as testifying all through to Him. All the more therefore the man who would be indeed the Lord's messenger, and not that poor counterfeit of that character, the preacher of his own ideas, must seek, pray, and watch against this fatal drift, and resolve, by faithful pains, to know his Bible. ("His Bible," I say on purpose, taking up the sweet old phrase which emphasizes the believer's personal relations to the blessed Book which his Redeemer loved and which in His resurrection-life He more than ever commended to His disciples.) Would we prepare to preach? We must not only choose a text and revive our acquaintance with its context; text and context must be to us living parts of that wonderful organism, the Holy Bible, multifold but vitally one, moved and moving all through with the Spirit of God. To the text we must bring the Bible. We must call in those "testimonies" which are "the men of our counsel," consulted not only for our sermons but for our souls, day by day.

So we shall be preparing continually for those inestimable little times (alas, how short they are in these days of hurry) which we are permitted to spend for Christ in the pulpit.  Our special preparation of the sermon will never ordinarily be superseded by this general preparation of the man ; but it will be incalculably altered by it, deepened, enriched, elevated, made capacious for the full blessing of the Lord.  By the mercy of God, we shall speak thoughtfully, soberly, in order, interestingly, so as to assist and command attention.  But above all, we shall speak as men who are the servants and companions of their King on the one hand, and their brethren on the other, and who come from Him to them to " speak that they do know, and to testify that they have seen."

# VII

By the REV. F. J. CHAVASSE, M.A.,
*Principal of Wycliffe Hall, Oxford.*

IT is impossible to discuss adequately in the limits here set so large a subject as preaching. I shall therefore confine myself to two questions.

1. What kind of sermons are especially needed at the present time to interest, instruct, and inspire our people?

2. How can we parochial clergy, who, for the most part, are men of average ability, who are distracted by unceasing calls, and who minister year after year to the same congregations, preach them?

I.—Three words describe the character of the preaching at which, I believe, we should aim. It should be extempore, expository, and systematic.

(1.) *Extempore.* The advantages of a written sermon are unquestionably many and great. The MS. ensures greater accuracy, more logical precision, more concise and well-balanced statements, and a better style. It adds greatly to the comfort of the preacher. It makes him independent of his digestion, and to a large extent of his health. It saves him from the humiliation and despair of uttering rash and foolish words, which he would give worlds to recall, and of seeing them carefully taken down by the hungry reporters under the pulpit. "It is easier to sleep on Saturday night with a sermon under his head than in it."

There are, moreover, times and places and congregations to which the written sermon is certainly the more appropriate.

Nevertheless, I believe, as a rule, with all its defects, the extempore sermon is more likely to be effective in the present day with the great mass of sermon hearers. It more readily secures attention. It is easier to deliver well; and with care and practice, I believe, it can be preached by most of us. It is the practice of the ministers of other Churches; why should the clergy of the English Church think it beyond their power?

(a) Now by extempore preaching I do not, of course, mean preaching without preparation, but without MS. More labour is probably involved in its cultivation, certainly at first, than need be bestowed upon the written sermon, and three rules must be carefully observed, which I will venture to call possession, arrangement, and self-forgetfulness.

1. *The Preacher must be possessed with his Subject.*—He must select it early in the week. He must make it his own by prayer, meditation, and reading. He must carry it about with him and let it slowly grow in his mind. He may talk it over with his sick, and in his pastoral visits to his people. He may gather material from his walks, and his casual conversations, from newspapers and magazines into which he dips, as well as in his hours of thought and reading in his study. It must be to him God's message to His people for that week, and he must be open to hear God's voices on every side. When at last his subject possesses him, he may be sure that it will reach and possess his hearers.

2. *He must carefully arrange his Matter.*—He will not only digest his materials, but he will mass them under clear, simple, and natural heads. Whether he gives his divisions to his people or not, he will keep them steadily before his own

mind. He will take care that they grow naturally and logically out of his subject, that they can be carried in his memory into the pulpit, and that his audience can carry them away to their own homes. "Without order in a sermon a preacher cannot get into his subject, and without order he cannot get out of it." One great secret of power in attracting and keeping attention lies in arrangement. If possible, the whole sermon should be mapped out in the introduction, and summed up again in the conclusion. Our hearers, when they grasp our outline, are prepared to follow us, and the summary at the close reminds them of some point they may have missed or forgotten. Ill-arranged sermons are intolerable to the cultured people in a congregation, and are unintelligible to the uneducated.

To secure this clear arrangement I believe it is well for the extempore preacher to write, if not at full length, at least the pith of what he has thought out. Writing promotes clearness of statement. It is a safeguard against irrelevancy. It incarnates, if I may so say, the floating visions of the brain, and helps us to see how they look when embodied in writing. Many a specious argument and many a fine idea, as it seemed at its inception, will not stand the sober test of being written out. "The best master of the orator is the pen." Writing not only stimulates thought, but it proves, clears, and compresses it.

The late Archbishop Magee recommended the clergy to write out a skeleton early in the week in clear and bold characters on a sheet of paper, and then to clothe the skeleton with words, remembering that they are writing a sermon and not an essay, with the people always before their mind. When the sermon is written out we are not to attempt to commit it to memory. Such a practice injures alike the health and brain of the preacher, and the usefulness of the sermon. He advises us to read over what we have written, and to make careful, clear, and short notes, writing out the line of thought, the chief divisions, and some sentences of the introduction and the conclusion, and to learn them by heart. Then to go through the sermon without the MS. This plan gives fulness, freedom of expression, and accuracy of thought. By degrees it will become necessary to write less and less, and I believe that to the last many of us will do well to write out a part at least of our sermon every week. The notes may or may not be taken up with us into the pulpit. They are of the greatest use in giving us confidence, and in impressing the subject on our mind; but the less we can use them the better. We shall never attempt to recall the exact words we have written down in our study. We shall trust to the spur of the moment for appropriate language. A true extempore speaker knows what he is going to say, but he does not know how he is going to say it. Mr. Pitt gave excellent advice to one of his contemporaries, "You are not as successful as you ought to be in the House of Commons, because you are more anxious about words than about ideas. If you are thinking of words you will have no ideas, but if you have ideas words will come of themselves."

3. *He must get rid of Self-Consciousness.*— The great foe of the extempore preacher is not nervousness but self-consciousness. Nervousness is a condition of success. We have all, I am sure, a vivid remembrance of our first attempt to speak in public without MS. We can still recall the sudden blank in memory, the dry throat, the

swimming head, the indistinct vision, the ardent desire for prompt and complete extinction. These are the heralds of future success. They indicate an excess of nerve-power—the power to impress an audience. No good speaker is free from nervousness. He loses with practice the excess, but to the last, as Martin Luther felt his knees knock together as he went up the steps of the pulpit, the preacher who reaches his people trembles as he faces them.

Self-consciousness is very different. It is a subtle form of pride which crushes inspiration, begets affectation, and destroys naturalness. The self-conscious preacher is either haunted by a fear that he will make a fool of himself, or he strains after effect. In either case he ceases to be natural, and forfeits his right and power to be effective. There is only one cure for self-consciousness, and that is love—love to God and to man. If we believe that we have a message to give, and that our message will help our hearers, we shall not think of ourselves. Self will be forgotten in the desire to benefit our people. And still more effectually self-consciousness is cured by God-consciousness. We are sent by God. We are His commissioned teachers. The Word we bear is not ours but His; and He is with us. In the realization of our commission, and of His Divine Presence, self passes out of sight.

(*b*) But while I believe that extempore preaching should be our aim, I do not mean that it is expedient that every young deacon fresh from the University, or even from a Theological College, should at once begin to preach extempore sermons in the parish church, but only that from the first he should educate himself to become an extempore preacher. I believe that with prayer and pains ninety-nine out of every hundred of our clergy may learn to speak acceptably without MS. There are many ways in which we can train ourselves.

1. By teaching in the day-school, and by catechizing in church. One half-hour spent daily, or even twice a week, in giving religious instruction to the children; a short twenty minutes spent on Sunday afternoon in giving a well-prepared catechetical address will form an invaluable training. We shall learn self-possession: how to think upon our legs; how to be simple, clear, and systematic; how to put the same idea in many ways, until we have made it plain; how to use

short and terse sentences, and to enforce our points by good illustrations. Some of us, as deacons, were apt to murmur that our vicars interpreted, as we thought too literally, the charge in the Ordination Service that we should "instruct the youth in the Catechism." I can only say that modern experience has proved the wisdom of the Church, and that as deacons we could not have a finer preparation for extempore preaching.

2. By speaking at Mission-room services and in the open air. In a freer and less formal atmosphere where the simplest and most elementary teaching is required, many a young preacher has acquired confidence, and has been trained to speak with clearness, directness, and force. One condition must, however, be severely borne in mind. We must respect and not despise our audience. Whether they be children or the poorest of the poor, we must prepare for them carefully and conscientiously. To say, "They are only children, or very uneducated, I can easily talk to them," and to give them the mere unpremeditated gush of perhaps a tired, or a shallow, or an unfurnished mind is a wrong. We are

giving to God, and to this people, what costs us nothing, and our sin sooner or later finds us out. It finds us out in a slovenly and slipshod style, from which it is exceedingly difficult to escape; in discourses marked by "a spoonful of thought in a riverful of words," in empty benches of listless hearers, and in inveterate habits which not only mar our pastoral preaching perhaps for life, but which leave their mark for evil on our ministerial character. "A sermon that costs us little trouble to compose, costs the people much to understand, and that which costs little is worth as much as it costs."

Yet, let me add, that if we are suddenly called upon to speak without preparation through no fault of our own, we may expect, without doubt, the fulfilment of our Lord's promise, " It shall be given you in that same hour what ye shall speak." Probably some of the most effective words spoken by many of us were uttered on the spur of the moment. The call to speak came to us unexpectedly and we obeyed it, relying upon the Master who called to give us our message, and our faith was not disappointed. God honours faith, but He dishonours indolence.

(II.) *Expository.*—There can be no question, I fear, that the Bible is not read and studied by the mass of our church-goers as it was fifty years ago, and that even amongst our more educated people the ignorance of its facts and teaching is deplorable. Into the causes of this grave feature of our modern Churchmanship I need not enter. It will be sufficient to notice that a measure of the blame lies with the clergy. Too little of our preaching has been calculated to interest our people in the Bible, and much of it has, I fear, tended to repel them from it. The atomical treatment of Holy Scripture, the preaching, I mean, upon isolated atoms or fragments of it, with little or no regard to the context; the practice of using a few Bible words as a motto upon which a sermon is hung, or in some cases which is hung upon the sermon as a kind of differentiating mark, has not helped forward the cause of Bible study. The still more reprehensible practice of what has been called, not inaptly, " Scripture conjuring," of extracting new, and unthought-of, and most ingenious interpretations from well-known passages of Holy Scripture, or of making less-read passages of Scripture bear hidden and spiritual meanings,—for instance, the description of the iron bedstead of Og, the wives of Solomon, and such like,—have repelled some minds from the Bible, and have caused others to regard it with a kind of despair as a book which can be interpreted and understood by a few ingenious and specially gifted people, but which is far beyond them. Happily, I think, we see the beginning of a healthier state of things. One result of the fire through which the Bible has passed and is passing is that we are learning to study its various books as a whole; to look at their statements in the light of the circumstances under which they were written, to grasp the great lessons they were meant to teach, to note the context, and to resent every attempt to put into any passage of Scripture a meaning it was never intended to bear. At the same time the minute, microscopical study of the Bible, which is also a feature of our time, is verifying the well-known saying of Stier, that "if we crumble up the Bible we find something in every crumb." We are coming to regard the Bible more and more as a text-book, and less and less as a book of texts.

With this widespread ignorance of the Bible amongst the masses and this juster and more minute knowledge amongst the few, it is our privilege, I believe, to carry the knowledge to the ignorant. Modern research has poured a flood of light upon the Bible. Its teaching inspires us as it never has done in the past. Our duty is to inspire others. I believe that we shall more surely interest our people in the Bible and inspire them with its spirit by preaching topical sermons less and expository sermons more; by giving them more of the thoughts of God and fewer of our own ideas. Chancellor Leeke, in his Pastoral Lectures at Cambridge (*Ourselves, Our People, Our Work*, p. 128), tells that when an undergraduate he heard the late Mr. Spurgeon preach one week-day afternoon in the old Chapel in St. Andrew's street. He cannot remember one word of his sermon, but his exposition he has never forgotten. Mr. Spurgeon read the sixteenth chapter of Numbers, the story of Korah, Dathan, and Abiram, with a short running commentary, and lighted up the chapter wonderfully. Why should not we do the same? How can we better bring home the truth of God to the hearts of our people than by "letting the Holy Scripture convey its message in its own words, with such explanation and comment as may be needful?" Why should not one, at least, of our sermons on Sunday be an exposition? Let the old and neglected practice be revived of the people following the preacher Bible in hand. Let a passage be carefully read through with short explanatory comments, and let one or two special lessons be pressed home, in conclusion, on the reason, the heart, and the conscience of our hearers. Two masters of such preaching we have amongst us at present in Dean Vaughan, and in Dr. Maclaren, the well-known Nonconformist minister of Manchester. This method has many advantages. It opens up large tracts of the Bible to our people. It teaches them to follow the argument and to grasp the lessons of a whole Book. It gives variety to our teaching, and ensures the treatment of many subjects which perhaps, if left to ourselves, we should have neglected. It obliges us to study systematically and diligently, with the best book we can find, a distinct portion of the Bible, and it preserves our preaching from becoming vague and narrow.

(III.) *Systematic.* — Another grave feature in modern Churchmanship is the absence of a systematic knowledge of Christian doctrine. We need only concern ourselves here with one of its causes

—the lack of orderliness and system in our preaching. Happily for us our Christian year ensures a certain amount of method, and is, in some measure, a defence against an unsystematic preacher. But even with the Christian year to guide us there is often a serious absence of orderly arrangement in the subjects of our sermons. By some of us no reference is ever made to the doctrine of the Atonement. By others the Sacraments are completely ignored. Some are for ever insisting upon doctrine to the exclusion of morality; others dwell on morality and seldom allude to doctrine. We need, I feel sure, to draw up, each man for himself, a course of systematic teaching, in which Christian doctrine and Christian ethics are brought before our people in a way suited to their intelligence. The Creeds, the Articles, and the Formularies of the Church if diligently studied will suggest the subjects, and at the beginning of each year we might select a certain number upon which to preach during the next twelve months.

The advantages of such a plan are great.

(a) The preacher will have topics for sermons ready to his hand. He will not be casting about, perhaps up to the last moment, for the subject upon which he is to preach. He will have good and thoughtful works of reference in which men who have been, or who are still, prophets in their own age, have given the Church their best and latest thoughts. He will be forced to study, and in trying to teach his people he learns himself. His own faith is strengthened, and many a difficulty is solved. Once finished, the course is a quarry out of which he can hew sermons for the rest of his life. He will add to it, perhaps modify some of its statements with the growth of knowledge and the decay of prejudice, but the pith of what he has written will remain the same.

(*b*) His people will hear the whole counsel of God, and be the better equipped against sin and error. They will listen to doctrinal sermons, which only cease to be a power when they are dead sermons, but which, when they come from a heart that has felt the living power of the truths they teach, and when they are made, as St. Paul made them, levers for higher and nobler living, are real sources of inspiration. The church-going laity as a whole do not, I am sure, object to dogmatic teaching. They only dislike the dogmatism which insists on the mere acceptance of a series of theological propositions which are never brought into line with the facts and needs of human life and experience; in other words, they resent the preaching of theological theories instead of living truths.

(*c*) They will be saved from sentimental sermons. Our hymns, our modern books of devotion, some of our religious newspapers and magazines, are too often ruined by sentimentality. Long-suffering congregations will tell you it has even forced its way into the pulpit. It may have attracted some women. It certainly has repelled many men. "Sentimentality," says one of the greatest preachers of the last twenty-five years, "disowns doctrine and it depreciates law. It asserts that religion belongs to feeling, and that there is no truth but love. The soft theology is worse than the hard." "Never rest," he adds, "till you touch men's brains and consciences. *Value no feeling which is not the child of truth and the father of duty.*"

By systematic preaching men will be reached. They will be morally and spiritually braced. They will be taught what they have to believe and how reasonable it is, and they will be shown how their faith can fashion their character and conduct, and make them like God.

## ON SERMON PREPARATION 141

II.—I pass on to ask, Is such preaching—extempore, expository, systematic—within the reach of our parochial clergy? I believe it is, in proportion as we endeavour to keep before our minds our Ordination vows and to be students, shepherds of our people, children of our age, and men of God.

1. *Students.*—We sometimes forget that at our ordination, not as deacon but as priest, when we had had every opportunity of realizing the claims and difficulties of the ministry, we deliberately promised, with God's help, to be diligent in three things—in prayer, in reading the Scriptures, and "in such studies as help to the knowledge of the same." Prayer, reading of the Bible, and study are linked together. All are equally binding upon us. And yet in how many cases does the busy and wearied parish priest, who would be shocked at the idea of ceasing to pray or to read his Bible, give up the idea of systematic study as altogether impossible?

Nevertheless, if we are to be preachers we must be students. The teacher must be a learner to the very end. Our University or Theological College course gave us more or less a start. But after all, there is much truth in the saying that "all that a man learns at a University is what he has to learn afterwards." Our University training teaches us to educate ourselves. Throughout all our life we must be learners; not mere readers, hastily skimming book after book, but students; men who read with a purpose; for "reading without purpose is sauntering, and not exercise." "Reading," said the late Professor Blackie (*Self-Culture*, p. 2), "in the case of miscellaneous readers is like the racing of some little dog about the moor snuffing everything and catching nothing. But a reader of the right sort finds his prototype in Jacob, who wrestled with an angel all night and counted himself the better for the bout, though the sinew of his thigh shrank in consequence."

Our reading should be Methodical, Particular, and yet General.

(*a*) *Methodical.*—While reading through the greater part of the Bible every year in the Lessons for the day, we should always have in hand some one book of the Old and New Testament which we should study with the same care with which we prepared our subjects for our University examinations. Let it be read if possible in the original, and with the best known commentary. Let our pen and note-book be in our hand, and let us write down the cream of the writer's ideas for future reference. For we are gathering materials which will prove invaluable for our sermons and for Bible-classes. Let us read with equal care some standard theological book, thoughtfully, and little at a time, and analysing as we go.

(*b*) *Particular*—We shall need as a rule to read specially for each sermon. Every subject should be thoroughly worked up. We are likely to have in our congregation some who are abler and better read than we are; but if we have carefully mastered our theme we shall be able to face them with a modest confidence that few, if any, have read more on that particular subject. "It was when the Prophet had built his altar, prepared the wood and laid the sacrifice in order that the fire of God descended upon it in answer to his prayer."

(*c*) *General*—" Our reading should be wider than our calling." When we are bidden to draw all our studies one way, it is their consecration not their limitation that is enjoined. The philosopher, the historian, the scientific and literary man will each find materials in his own department for enriching his sermon and teaching his people. It is well, if possible, to have one book on our desk which does not bear directly on theology. It will add freshness and breadth and reality to our preaching.

But how, it may be asked, can the busy parochial clergy find time to be students? Something, I think, may be done by self-denial and method.

By early rising we may secure an hour or more before breakfast. One hour a day given to a particular subject until it is mastered will yield an astonishing harvest at the end of twelve months. And the secret of early rising is early going to bed. If only the time often wasted at night after our work is finished in aimless dawdling were only given to sleep, many a precious hour would be won in the early morning for vigorous and fruitful study. If a Wesleyan student, by the rules of his society, is bound to be in his study at six a.m., why should we English clergy be too often found in our beds an hour, or even two hours, later?

By resolutely setting aside a part at least of our mornings after breakfast and refusing to be interrupted. The busy doctor names certain hours daily at which he can be found at home, and his patients have to come to him at those times. Why do we allow our time to be broken up into small fragments in which it is all but impossible to read, when with a little firmness and management we might secure at least two hours of uninterrupted quiet? The fact is that sometimes we find hard reading and steady thought less congenial than a conversation with an interesting parishioner, or an interview with a zealous worker, or a stroll into the parish. Certainly in the earlier days of our ministerial life most of us might secure some time every day for study as well as for prayer and reading the Bible.

By using fragments of time. Charles Kingsley notes how much can be done by utilizing for reading odd quarters of an hour. A well-known Dean has, it is said, re-written at least one book in the interval between family prayers and breakfast. If a book were always at hand, many a few minutes, now perhaps wasted in re-scanning a well-read newspaper, might be well employed in gathering materials for next Sunday's sermon, or in adding to our stock of knowledge in doctrine or history.

Prebendary Gibson, in his excellent lectures on "Self-discipline," tells of a clergyman who, deeply impressed at a Quiet Day by the duty to study, went home and told his wife that, though he had always tried to do his best as a parish priest, he had never realized so keenly before that study was a duty incumbent upon him, and that for the future he would set apart some time every day for reading. Within a year he was called to his rest, and his parishioners, knowing nothing of his resolution, said that the last few months of his ministry were more fruitful than all that had gone before. His sermons had gained in force, and the flame of his own spiritual life seemed to burn more brightly than ever. Those who knew him well put it down to the resolution which he had made, and which he had faithfully striven to keep.

2. *Shepherds of our people.*—Preaching has been defined as "the communication of truth through men to men." A preacher needs something more than the knowledge of the best books. He must know human nature. None but one who knows men can speak to men. We may learn much about men from books. St. Chrysostom, whose knowledge of character was remarkable, was a diligent student of Aristophanes. A thorough acquaintance with a great dramatist like Shake-

speare, or a great allegory like "The Pilgrim's Progress," will help us to preach with much greater force. We shall learn even more by knowing our own heart. "I know men," Massillon used to say, "because I know myself." But we shall learn most by knowing our people. A parochial preacher must be a pastor. He cannot preach so as to reach his flock without sympathy, and sympathy involves personal knowledge of those with whom we sympathize. It is as we move about amongst our people, learning their peculiar circumstances, temptations, difficulties, and sorrows, that we learn how to speak to them from the pulpit with point. It is likely, and it is very desirable, that before very long we shall have in many of our dioceses a special company of preachers composed of men who have special gifts of utterance, who will relieve the overworked parochial clergy by taking from them a part of their preaching. It will, I think, be a mistake if a fast and hard line be drawn between the preacher and the pastor. The pastor who has no preaching is likely to lose some at least of his realization of the dignity of his office, and certainly some of its highest joys, and the preacher who is no pastor is in danger of losing his sympathy, and of becoming indefinite and theoretical. I am sure that what our people need are not weekly orations, but teaching and counsel; not eloquence or learning, but simple, thoughtful, sympathetic sermons, which teach them in a language they can understand how to serve God in their daily lives, how to meet sorrow and to resist sin, and how to help their fellowmen. Therefore, in thinking, reading, or writing, a preacher must always have his people before him. His subject, his language, his style, his illustrations, must be adapted to their capacities. " If we forget that we have to preach to a congregation, we shall have no congregation to preach to." We must seek for inspiration in the souls of our people. " Non sumus Oratores sed Piscatores." The late John Bright once expressed his surprise that any man could preach week after week to the same congregation. The task is difficult, and had we to prepare a weekly oration the difficulty for many of us would be insuperable. But when we know our people, and love and respect them, love and knowledge open our hearts and unseal our lips. We find some of our best sermons in the houses of our parishioners. Our talks with them open up unexpected avenues of thought and methods of application. We never, of course, betray their confidences; but we learn what are their present needs, and rightly divide for them the word of truth. We learn how they think and speak. In the country, and perhaps in the town, the vocabulary of the poor is much smaller than ours. Too often our sermons are preached in a tongue not understood of the people, and our illustrations are incorrect or unsuitable. The late Dr. Heurtley, intending to preach to a country congregation on "the Brazen Serpent," wisely asked beforehand as he visited, whether his villagers knew what a serpent was. None had any conception. But a snake was intelligible; and about the Brazen Snake he preached.

Bishop Dupanloup recommended his clergy to give from time to time simple and familiar addresses in which they spoke to their flocks as a father would speak to his children. "We should tell them," he says, "all that we have in our hearts, for or against them." I think that certainly in the country such quiet fatherly talks would be invaluable. They would need, as he points out, careful preparation. They must be given in dignified though simple language. Then they would help to bridge over any chasm that exists between pulpit and pew. They would teach our people to regard us as their counsellor and friend, and to regard themselves more as members of our family and less as isolated units in a congregation.

Yet there are dangers to which an intimate knowledge of our people may expose us. We may become too minute in our teaching. We may begin to lose faith in certain articles of the Creed because they do not seem to help at the moment our particular flock. It is, therefore, good for us to preach from time to time to congregations in which we do not know a face. Then, our own little parish and our peculiar worries and difficulties are lost in the needs and claims of humanity. Then our view of truth, which perhaps was becoming somewhat contracted, grows larger again and our sense of failure is forgotten. Then the nobility of our calling is brought home to us with renewed force. We feel that Christ's Gospel is a message to mankind in general, and not to our own people alone.

3. *Children of our age.*—Bishop Carpenter, in

his suggestive book on "Preaching," quotes a saying of Schiller:—"The poet should be the child of his age, but woe to him if he be its favourite or its slave." What is true of the poet is equally true of the preacher. He ought to be a prophet to his people, unfolding the will of God as they need and are able to bear it; interpreting passing events, and elucidating the purposes of God. It is for us to watch, in an age of movement and turmoil, the currents of human thought and feeling, and to leaven and to guide them by proclaiming the great principles of truth and righteousness which God has committed to His Church. We are not to be afraid of, or ashamed of, or to despair of our age. It is neither worse nor better than those that have gone before. It has, as they had, its special difficulties, tendencies, temptations, failures, and successes. And we are not to be living on the traditions of the past, and to be looking back regretfully to a supposed golden age, which is probably golden only in imagination; but we are to seek to serve our own generation by trying to understand its needs and to meet them. If we believe, as we do, that Christianity is Divine, we may be sure that it has a mission and a message to a scientific, democratic, practical, but not irreligious time like ours. We have no right to be afraid of science or of any modern "ism," whether it be socialism or criticism, nor impulsively to give in our adhesion to all that is put forward in their behalf out of reverence for some great and justly-honoured name. We need courage and discrimination and self-control. We shall be ready to sympathize with and to encourage every high and noble aspiration after truth and righteousness, but we shall not rashly embrace every new theory, and startle and unsettle our people by light-hearted denunciations of what we think their narrow, unscientific, uncritical, and selfish opinions. Nor on the other hand shall we hastily brand as infidel or irreligious, those who have formed opinions contrary to our own on some of the burning questions of the day. Our preaching must be constructive and not destructive. It is not our business to preach scientific, political, and critical sermons, but to give the message of God to men's souls. "We are to do our threshing in the study, and give our people the wheat, and to keep the chaff out of the pulpit." We have to witness to the changeless amid the changing, and to the permanent amid the perishable. Men's consciences and hearts are much the same in every age, and we have to help them in their daily battle with sin and sorrow and unbelief, with the message which our Lord has committed to us. Let science, and politics, and criticism be kept to their proper places; in the Church let us go and preach the kingdom of God.

At the same time we shall take care that we live in the present, and not in the past, that the vices we rebuke are present-day vices, and the difficulties we seek to meet present-day difficulties, that the message we give is one by which men can live in the closing years of the nineteenth century, and not one better suited for a generation which has passed away. The Gospel, indeed, never changes, but different ages need to have it presented in a different form, and call for the special prominence of different doctrines. The spirit of our teaching from first to last should be wholly Scriptural, but the body in which it is clothed should take its form from the age in which we live.

To this end let us study men, newspapers, biographies, and all that will show us what our people and our time are thinking about. Relevancy and opportuneness add great power to pastoral preaching.

4. *Men of God.*—Yet it avails us little to be students, shepherds of our people, children of our age, unless we are also *Men of God*. The reason is obvious. "The two great elements in preaching are," as Bishop Phillips Brooks reminds us, "personality and truth." The truth must come through the man and not over him. We shall be as preachers what we are as men. Sir F. Leighton's maxim as to artists is equally true of clergymen, "As we are, so is our work." None but the pure in heart can see the vision of God, or effectively deliver His message. The careless, prayerless, self-indulgent clergyman may proclaim the truth, but there is no ring of sincerity in his words, and no power of consistency in his life. Men listen and may praise, but their character and conduct are alike untouched. It is not merely that inconsistency mars the message of the preacher, but unspirituality incapacitates him from fully grasping and expressing the truth; and his words lack the life that carries them like winged shafts into the hearts and consciences of his hearers. He has no real moral

affinity with God, and therefore fails to represent Him. Well may George Herbert sing—

> "O what pure things, most pure, must those things be
> Who bring my God to me."

It has been well said that " the three gifts which make a great preacher in all times and countries are the *sympathy* which can move and lift the hearers, the *insight* into spiritual facts which can present them as luminous realities, and the *enthusiasm* for a sacred cause which can fire the soul with a congenial devotion." And these only come in their highest and most lasting form when we walk with God.

The tenderest, strongest, noblest *sympathy* is the outcome of loving God. We find the pattern, the motive, and the power to love our people in the fact that God loves us and them, and sends us as His representatives to shepherd and to help them. Time, opposition, intimate knowledge, ingratitude, indifference may kill the sympathy that flows from a meaner source, but, like the spring of an unfailing stream which lies too deep for the touch of the summer sun or of winter frosts, they cannot hurt the sympathy that wells up from a heart that has learned to love God because God first loved him.

*Insight* into textual criticism, into historical environment, into theological subtleties may be won by a strong brain and by unwearied study, but the keenest intellect and the most massive learning cannot transform "spiritual facts into luminous realities." That is the gift of God the Holy Spirit alone, and it is given only to those who wait upon God in a life of prayer, meditation, and unselfishness. Such men see light in God's light, and come down from the mount transfigured and inspired to speak what they have seen and heard and know.

Natural *enthusiasm* soon dies down in the ministerial life. We go out in our new armour dreaming of easy and universal conquest. In a few years we become, as we think, wiser men, and cease to attempt the impossible, and are content to live as other men live, and to fail where others failed before us. But he who has the Divine enthusiasm which comes from having God in him, who honours the presence and work of God the Holy Spirit, who is content to "lose himself to save himself," and who lives near God, he unconsciously inspires others because God inspires him. He has learned those things which have burned themselves into his soul, and which, so long as he lives near God, will never lose their power over his life—the greatness of God, the value of a soul, the awfulness and the glory of the ministry committed to his charge. Such men may not possess great ability, or learning, or eloquence, but they are powers. Their words may be simple, but the man behind the words lends them force, and the Spirit of God carries them home. They speak as God's messengers. They themselves are lost in their message, and their people recognize them as prophets of God.

At no time in the history of our Church had the pulpit greater influence than at present. Men will come to hear sermons delivered without book, opening out what they believe to be the Word of God and unfolding His whole counsel. They ask only that the preacher shall not give what has cost him nothing, but what has been gathered by honest study, by intercourse with his people, by the observance of his times, and by constant communion with God. It is not what are called great sermons that tell, but, as Bishop Phillips Brooks says, "the sermons of which nobody speaks, which come from mind and heart to go to heart and mind with as little consciousness, as possible, of tongue and ear—these are the sermons that do the work, that make men better men, and really sink into their affections. They are like the perfect days when no man says, 'How fine it is,' but every man does his best work and feels most fully what a blessed thing it is to live."

A master hand has drawn for us the picture of the pattern preacher. In proportion as we are men of God we shall reproduce it. "This was the fashion of it : it had eyes lifted up to heaven ; the best of books in its hands ; the law of truth was written on its lips ; the world was behind its back ; it stood as it pleaded with men, and a crown of gold did hang over its head."

# VIII

By the REV. H. W. WEBB-PEPLOE, M.A.,
*Vicar of St. Paul's, Onslow Square, and Prebendary of St. Paul's Cathedral.*

No man who has been preaching several times in the week almost without cessation for more than thirty years, can truthfully say that he is "unaccustomed to public speaking," or claim indulgence on the ground of his "utter inexperience." So that if required to tell the unvarnished tale of one's workshop, the best thing is perhaps to let "I" come straight out, and speak the whole truth.

At the time that I took my degree at Cambridge (1859) there was little or no assistance given to young men by the authorities of the University in their preparation for the tremendous task of preaching. In fact nothing was really done to fit them in any way for the practical duties of the ministry. Their theological training was of the most meagre and perfunctory description; and as for elocution, sermon making, and pastoral duties, men were left absolutely without instruction from those who had charge of their education. A certain amount of practical work was, of course, being done through the Jesus-lane Sunday-school and through tract distribution in the villages; but these were simply the outcome of individual earnestness and zeal, and, so far as I knew, were permitted, not pressed upon us, as fields for the display of personal energy. I entered upon both of these during my first term at college; but owing to a severe accident at the commencement of my second term's residence, I had to spend the rest of my Cambridge career on my back, and could not therefore take part in these active forms of preparation for the ministry. But during my last year I joined a small voluntary class of men, each of whom undertook to write a sermon during the Vacation, and to deliver the same during the following term before the other members of the class, who, after the delivery, were to criticize it freely (in writing and anonymously), the remarks of all being read aloud by one of the hearers. This would, of course, be very helpful if done regularly and with much prayer; but I had only the benefit of writing one sermon for the class, and can well remember that it received ample criticism from my friends.

My next experience in sermon preparation was to find myself ordained, and in sole charge—though still but a deacon—of a large parish in Herefordshire (the Vicar, my father, being non-resident, and in charge of a parish some four miles distant). In this sphere I had also the charge of the workhouse, of which I was chaplain. I had, therefore, from the very commencement of my ministry, to supply at least three (and often four or more) sermons every week; and from that time forward I seldom, if ever, had less; while, naturally, for the last eighteen years in London I have had to supply a much larger number at times.

I mention these facts to encourage my younger brethren, who sometimes speak as if the duty of furnishing one or two discourses in a week were altogether beyond a young man's possibility; and not unmindful of the stringent rules laid down upon this subject for deacons by His Grace the Archbishop of York, who seems to think that no young man can rightly do more than make one sermon a month which is to be called *his own*.

It is quite possible for a young man to have too much—but I humbly think that he may also have too little—of sermon production. But upon what conditions may he hope to make many sermons with profit? Upon exactly the same conditions as any other young man must observe who hopes in these days to succeed in his profession, viz. that he be willing to work almost day and night without ceasing; to be (not merely to be talked of as) the man of "one thing" like St. Paul; to "give attendance to reading, to exhortation, to doctrine"; to meditate upon these things, to give himself wholly to them, and above all "take heed to *himself*" that his whole being and life be absorbed in that business to which he is pledged, and which more than any other on earth requires *the whole man* for its success. To make new sermons every week the man must be yearning over souls; must be night and day laid hold of by the conviction that men are perishing, and will perish for ever if he do not so give them God's Word, as to awaken them from their awful position, and save them from the eternal destruction which awaits them if they continue to sleep the sleep of death. To preach fresh sermons for thirty or forty years requires, I believe, the ever-present power, and the precious workings of God the Holy Ghost in a man's soul; so that, while the labour is intense, the "travail" "an agony," and the strain unending in every department of the preacher's being, yet the power is given and the freshness provided (that freshness being of course spiritual, far more than mental or literary), because the food supplied to the people is not human, but Divine. I confess that the strain was very great in my youth, but I do not know that it has ever appeared less, at all events spiritually; for it seems to me that a sermon produced without real spiritual "travailing in birth for one's children" in the faith, is not a sermon at all; but a meal of husks and dry bones for the people.

In the earliest days of my ministry I wrote my two Sunday sermons from beginning to end; and then reading them over twice on Saturday and Sunday, so committed them to memory that I did not need (I believe) to refer to my MS. at all. This would be to some even a wearisome labour, and cannot, I think, be considered a wise step for any man to adopt, if he proposes to continue it, or if he is a slave to his own sentences. I had no one to criticize me in my youth (being never in the position of a curate); but I have certainly discovered one or two brethren in this habit, and consider its adoption to be dangerous in every way, as producing a stiff and stilted delivery, and as sure to have its revenge upon the man himself, when he happens to be weak, and in physical or mental distress. My workhouse and school-room addresses were from the first made from notes which were carefully and elaborately framed.

The only criticism that I remember being passed upon my preaching during the first year or two of my ministry was that of the old village schoolmistress, who had known me from a boy, and I never understood whether it was a word of praise or condemnation: " Well, you have got one gift, at all events—the gift of the gab!" This was owing to a habit which young men should watch, and which has, I fear, been a hindrance in some ways (if helpful in others) to myself, viz. the habit of pouring out my words, whether written or extempore, very rapidly, though with my whole heart thrown into them, I hope, at all times. This habit I may have unconsciously adopted from my uncle, Capel Molyneux, who at the opening of my ministry came to visit my parents, and preached for me in the Church of Weobley, where I was in sole charge. I remember well his sermon, which was on Mal. iii. 18. It was almost the only time I ever heard him preach, and for fifty minutes he poured forth his words of invitation, counsel, warning, and instruction. It would be considered far too long a sermon now; but it made a deep impression by its spirituality and earnestness then.

And how did he, a great preacher in his own way, prepare? I asked him as we walked from the church that day, and I well remember all that he said. "I read almost nothing but my Bible, and from that I really prepare my sermons, with almost no other helps." "But," I said, "upon what books, &c., have you framed your style?" "Upon almost none," he said; "but if upon any, I suppose I should say upon Dwight's *Theology.*" Thereupon I bought Dwight and meditated and studied him well, but I am bound to say that (like Simeon's *Skeletons*) I have always felt that, though very systematic and a fruit of much labour, "the bones were very dry" indeed, and that a little of such "systems" would go a long way with our hearers, more especially in these days of impatience and haste. Still it would unquestionably be well for most congregations if the preachers of the present day were allowed to preach much less often, and to take some such pains as Mr. Molyneux seems to have taken. I have heard from two gentlemen who possess large stores of his sermons that the form of preparation is most elaborate, each sermon being produced in at least three different forms—(1) carefully and almost fully written out; (2) reduced to a short digest, like a single sheet; and (3) reduced again to the mere heads on a small slip, which was taken into the pulpit.

From Mr. Molyneux (I think) it was that I heard of a famous "Golden Lecturer" of the last generation who used to give thirty-six hours to the preparation of each sermon. Oh, for the days of quiet and retirement which the preacher of those days must have known! Would it be good or bad for the nation if we could go back to them? I cannot say. But to take things as they stand and to convey my own rules—circumstances and hard work have produced all that I have or am; and I humbly thank God for my measure of unmerited success.

I.—In regard to choice of subject and text. How thankful the Church of England clergy should be for the rota of our services which year by year force upon our own and our people's attention all the most solemn subjects—historical, doctrinal, and practical—which it is the minister's duty to bring before his people. For many years I have almost always found my text in the lessons or other parts of the service for each particular Sunday, and yet there is always something "new" in the "old treasures." Of course there will be exceptional occasions when special texts must be chosen, but it is remarkable to observe the supply and the variety which are provided in the different parts of the services as arranged for us by our Church.

How different is the experience of our Nonconformist brethren, and how difficult must be the task imposed upon them of choosing passages of Scripture for reading and texts for sermons without reference to particular seasons or subjects. This is well expressed (though unconsciously perhaps) by the late Dr. Dale in the preface to his volume recently published, *Christian Doctrine*, where he says:—" To avoid the danger of failing to give to any of the great doctrines of the

Christian faith an adequate place when preaching, I have sometimes drawn up in December or January a list of some of the subjects on which I resolved to preach during the following twelve months." He then gives one of his lists, which only contains the very truths which we, as clergy of the Church of England, are called to bring before our people year by year; and what is this but to confess a tendency which all must feel to cleave to particular subjects to the exclusion of others, and to say that we may well be thankful for a service book and arrangements of lessons, which call upon us to treat all these subjects in turn? So far, then, as regards the choice of texts, I believe that it is manifestly our duty and wisdom to follow very much the lines which our own Church has laid down, and so treat every great subject of God's Revelation in turn.

II.—The texts being chosen as early as possible in the week (on the Sunday evening if possible, before the week's work begins), how shall the real work of preparation be performed?

(1) By humble, earnest prayer for light, guidance, and wisdom in the whole conduct of the matter.

(2) By seeking to shape out the lines and objects of the sermon.

(3) By close study of the passage and all that bears on it in God's Word.

(4) By writing as freely as possible one's own thoughts on the subject.

(5) By then, and not till then, reading other men's treatment of the passage.

(6) Then re-shaping one's own MS., if needful, from what one has learned.

(7) So gathering up the whole subject into the brain and heart, that one is really master thereof (so far as one's powers extend), and prepared to deliver it as one's own message for the Lord.

III.—Whether there should be always divisions and subdivisions; and whether these should be made visible to the congregation, have always been disputed points. My own opinion is that for the preacher himself there cannot be too much care expended upon the heads or divisions; but that it is not generally wise to express them all to the hearers; and yet I am often told (more especially by the Scotch) that " they prefer a discourse in which the heads are announced." The objection to such an announcement seems to be that it prevents the hearers from forgetting the *man*, but at the same time it certainly helps them to remember his *points*.

Monsieur Claude (whose famous essay upon "The Composition of a Sermon" was translated from the French in 1778 by the Rev. Robert Robinson, a dissenting minister in Cambridge) lays it down that "There are, in general, *five* parts of a sermon—the exordium, the connection, the division, the discussion, and the application—but that connection and division are parts which ought to be extremely short, and we may properly reckon, therefore, only *three* parts in a sermon."

Mr. Simeon, who made much use of Claude's essay, tells us that he "considers three things as indispensably necessary in any discourse—*unity* in the design, *perspicuity* in the arrangement, and *simplicity* in the diction." "The language," he says, "ought certainly to rise with the subject, but it is a vicious task to be aiming at what is called fine language; the language should not elevate the subject, but the subject it."

Here we have, surely, right sound advice. And here we venture a word, perhaps, on

IV.—The delivery of sermons without MS. or

note, which is often described as "extempore preaching." If this term were lightly applied to my own custom in this matter, I should consider that I was guilty of a grievous sin towards God, and of a positive insult to my hearers. The late Archbishop of York (Dr. Magee), in his lectures to young men at the Chapter-house, St. Paul's, used (as I remember reading it in the papers) this expression: "True extempore speaking is either a necessity or a crime," and then proceeded to explain that if done by that necessity (*i.e.* a call of God at any moment), we might expect that the Almighty would enable us, and would deign to bless the act of obedience and faith; but that, if done under the idea that we might at any time trust the Spirit, it was simply a cloak or excuse for laziness, and would be sin.

With this wise utterance I would wish to express my hearty agreement, and I am the more constrained to express my opinion in this matter, because in *The A B C of Public Speaking* the author has deigned to honour me with a special notice, as one who "speaks under inspiration for which the preparation is *nil.*" Thank God if the words have any—even the smallest—appearance of inspiration; but let me say that I have *always* considered it my duty to give long hours of preparation (the more given the better) to every sermon that I am called to deliver. Though I very soon abandoned the habit of writing sermons out fully, and early adopted the custom of showing no MS. or notes, I may honestly say that through all the days and *nights* of the week I am seeking to prepare for the holy office of *preaching*—and why? This brings me to the last point on which I may now venture to speak.

V.—What should be the subject of all Christian men's sermons? Without hesitation I answer "Jesus Christ and Him crucified," *i.e.* not of course the one ceaseless iteration of the truth, however precious and powerful — " Behold the Lamb of God which taketh away the sins of the world," but so bringing forth Jesus Christ the Saviour in every discourse, that no sinner can pass away without hearing how his soul may be saved, and no troubled or tempted one can go forth and say, "That Gospel does not meet *my* needs."

"I'll preach as though I ne'er should preach again,
And as a dying man to dying men."

These lines were sent to me anonymously, soon

after I came to work in London, and over the chimney-piece in our vestry they have been, as I hope, an inspiration to myself and to others for years. Every time that we are called to preach, what have we to deliver but the Gospel of Jesus Christ? Surely, then, in our preparation or in our delivery there should be the perpetual remembrance and realization of this fact, "Men's everlasting destinies will hang upon the words which I shall be uttering when this sermon is preached"; and with this solemn thought pressing in upon the soul, I do not understand how any man can do less than (1) "Pray without ceasing" for God's blessing on his words, (2) "Give himself wholly" to this greatest work of his life, (3) "Take heed to himself" that his profiting may appear unto all men, and (4) "Continue in the doctrine committed to his trust, avoiding profane babblings and oppositions of science falsely so-called"—knowing that "by doing this he shall both save himself and them that hear him."

# IX

By the Rev. W. Hay M. H. Aitken.

I SUPPOSE that no preacher, whether "great" or otherwise, comes up to his own ideal; but it is often nothing less than humiliating to feel how far in one's own judgment one seems to come short of it. Still, if we can help each other to never so slight an extent, we ought not to allow ourselves to be deterred from doing so by any consciousness of our own shortcomings.

The thought that has influenced me more than, perhaps, any other in my preaching for long years past has been this, that preaching always should "mean business"; and I am bound to say that in the few cases in which I have an opportunity of hearing voices other than my own the conclusion is not unfrequently forced upon me that this guiding principle has only been very imperfectly apprehended, if apprehended at all. A sermon may be awakening, or evangelizing, or didactic, or hortative, or exegetical, or topical, or doctrinal, and in each of these cases the preacher may "mean business" and effect what he is aiming at; but when we have exhausted our powers of classification there remains the largest group of all, which, I am afraid, we must needs designate nondescript. Is there an equal promise of "business" in these? or is the effect likely to be as nondescript as the sermon?

The preacher is God's advocate, and his pleadings should surely have at least as much purpose in them as the business utterances of the Bar. In rare cases I believe lawyers have been known to "plead against time"; yet even then they have an object. But what shall be said of the preacher who contrives to convey to his hearers the idea that this is his object? Surely it is not by "speaking against time" that our case is to be carried! Have your point well in view from the first; "grow towards your point"; press your point home; expect to carry your point—these would be my words of counsel to any younger brother who was anxious to become an effective preacher. A sermon should be like a barbed arrow, and it will be none the worse for carrying a good many barbs. But one sometimes hears a sermon that makes one think of an arrow with barbs indeed, and these unduly elongated, but all alike turned the wrong way. Let the reader take the trouble to present these two figures to the "faithful eye" on paper, with some slight exaggeration of detail, such as would hardly present itself naturally to one's mind in connection with archery, and the diagram that he will produce will afford him an impressive illustration of the difference between an effective and a futile sermon.

In the one case the preacher, starting with a definite object before his mind, will possibly introduce both solid matter and illustration which may not at first sight seem wholly germane to his subject; but these accretions to the original theme will be of a kind to catch the hearer's attention, or to deepen it if already caught, while they will all ultimately lead towards the point, just as at one time all roads were said to lead to Rome, and will enable the point to infix itself all the more firmly in the hearer's heart.

In the other case the preacher sets forth with no more definite object than the preaching of a sermon; the thing has to be done, and he is the man that has to do it. He starts, we will suppose, along some well-defined line of thought; but before he has gone far an inviting digression leads him into a by-path which he pursues with the result of finding himself in a veritable *cul de sac*. From this he escapes by a somewhat abrupt return to his original theme, which breaks the continuity of his discourse and fatigues the attention of the hearers. By the time two or three more inverted barbs have been attached the arrow is pretty well warranted not to fly, or at any rate not to fly straight or swiftly, and then comes the crowning stroke of unwisdom, when at last you reach the place where the point ought to be,—instead of a point you find something that puts you in mind of a toasting-fork, you cannot say which of the straggling ends of the sermon is to take precedence of its brother stragglers; and you go out of the church with a confused sensation that you have heard a good deal but really don't know what it was all about. Such sermons may do good, for God may see that the underlying intention was sound, even if the method was unskilful, and our all too frequent blunders do not limit His power of blessing; but none the less the wonder is that sermons of this order should prove profitable, not that they should be a beating of the air.

I am persuaded that our admiration of great preachers frequently leads our younger clergy away from a reasonable and business-like view of preaching to a very unbusiness-like, sometimes an unreasonable attempt at imitation of that which in our pulpit heroes we most admire. A prominent Wesleyan preacher related to me some years ago the following incident. A worthy man who was in charge of a congregation in connection with that body, was, I may say, the victim of an incontinent admiration for the great Methodist orator, Morley Punshon. His one idea in his ministerial work was to preach like Mr. Punshon, the man he admired, and with a view to this he laboriously wrote and re-wrote his sermon, worked up his periods with the greatest care; but with all his pains, somehow or other, the reproduction of the great preacher never seemed to come off. Either his memory failed at some critical point, or the thing that looked well on paper sounded inflated or unnatural, and by humiliating experiences he had the sad fact brought more and more home to him to his intense chagrin that he was, to use an

ON SERMON PREPARATION 179

expression that has almost become proverbial, "grasping at the stars and sinking in the mud!" Meanwhile, his ministry seemed destitute of all spiritual success, he could not even keep up his congregation, and his heart sank within him as he contemplated his futile toil.

While things were thus going from bad to worse with him, it happened that an opportunity was offered him of hearing the great American Evangelist, Mr. Moody. He gladly availed himself of it and sat night after night, like one astonished, listening to the direct and business-like utterances of this most successful of soul-winners. On returning to his wife he was met with the question, " Well, what do you think of the great preacher?" " Preacher," he exclaimed, " why he doesn't preach at all! He just stands there and talks, as if he were only having an earnest conversation with a single individual, although he has got 7000 before him, and the people just seem to feel that he means every word that he says, and they crowd forward by the hundred to give themselves to God. I tell you what it is, I've done with Morley Punshon for ever! From this time forward I'm going to see whether I can't talk too." And the next Sunday he did "talk." It was not that he now attempted to imitate a new hero, where he had lost faith in the old; it was that he had laid aside all attempts at becoming even a considerable preacher of the conventional type; he was fired with a new enthusiasm and inspired with a new sense of reality in his work, and God was with him. A work of grace began there and then under his ministry that led up to such great things that some four years later, when I had my talk with this friend, he had already been instrumental in setting on foot work in no less than fifteen Mission centres, in each of which souls were being won for Christ and the lost were being reclaimed.

I have not related this story in order to cast a slur on the memory of one of the most eloquent preachers of the century. Mr. Punshon had his own particular gifts, and did well in making such a brilliant use of them. He would have been just as ill advised in copying Mr. Moody's methods as Mr. Moody would have been in copying his. Our own great preacher Liddon had a unique position to fill, and he filled it to good purpose. The Church of Christ has need of such gifts, and her Master bestows them upon her according to

His own sovereign wisdom; but to only few in each generation is such a part assigned, and he who aspires to it must have good reason to believe that this is his special calling. If it be so he will be no mere imitator. If he is to be a great preacher, God will endow him with that genuine originality which is the condition of such greatness, and which cannot be stimulated by any imitative process whatsoever.

"Naturalness" I conceive to be one of the most certain conditions of effective preaching, and it is a characteristic to which young preachers should give their most serious attention. A stilted and conventional style, an attempt at rhetorical expression, where there is not the art to conceal art; above all, a mannerism in delivery which is put on as soon as the preacher enters the pulpit, very much as the Greek actors put on their masks before they appeared on the stage—all these are barriers to success in preaching, which only extraordinary ability can enable the preacher to surmount. The nearer that we get to speaking in the pulpit as we do out of it, the more likely are we to be listened to. Above all, our young preachers need to be warned against a monotonous sing-song.  I am inclined to think that some preachers that I have listened to would have been more effective if they had sung their sermons outright to a Gregorian tone.  The novelty of such a procedure might at any rate for a time have attracted attention, where the unmusical cadences, not less determinate than if they had been musical, only had the effect of inducing somnolence.

If the monotone is to follow us from the desk into the pulpit, only varied there by mournful and exasperating inflexions, the sooner we bar it the better.  But why should this be so?  Commonsense should teach us that while Almighty God is not affected by the tone of our voice one way or another, our fellow-men are, and that, therefore, what may be justifiable for certain obvious reasons in the one case cannot be excused in the other.

Side by side with "naturalness" in expression and deliverance I would insist on the importance of a concrete habit of thought.  Of course it is impossible wholly to dispense with abstractions, nor is it desirable that we should do so, but the habit of throwing everything into a more or less abstract form is a besetting vice of the clerical mind, and tends to give our utterances a transcendental tone that militates grievously against their effectiveness. It is frequently easier, and sometimes much less unpleasant, to deliver our message in abstract terms than to condescend to details. A conventional acquaintance with popular theology enables us to use the proper and time-honoured phrases, which seem to be what are expected from a preacher's lips. But in order to deal with man as he is, and with truth and falsehood, sin and righteousness, as they exist in relation to him, we need carefully to study the facts of the case.

Probably our most effective sermons will be those that are suggested by our personal dealings with our fellow-sinners. The objections that are raised, the excuses that are offered, the doubts that are flaunted as it were in our face to frighten us from the exercise of our friendly offices, the sophistries with which men dupe their consciences, the refuges of lies behind which they attempt to shield themselves from conviction, all these are so many providentially given texts, from which we may expect so to preach that our word shall go home. And these are not the only kind of concrete facts that we shall find ourselves brought face to face with in our study of men as we find them. We shall discover allies as well as foes in every human heart, and we shall be all the more likely to touch the sympathies, and stir the hearts of men when we recognize the good as well as the evil that exists within.

As to the methods that I myself employ, I do not claim any special merit for these, at least not for the most of them. I am an extempore preacher in this sense, that I trust to the inspiration of the moment for the words in which to clothe the ideas already furnished to my mind by such careful antecedent preparation as I am able to make. My notes are usually contained on a single half-sheet of note-paper, somewhat closely written. To this outline I usually adhere with considerable fidelity, but at the same time I hold myself free to modify by additions or omissions in the course of delivery as I feel myself led. Things sometimes wear a different aspect in the pulpit from what they did in the study, and the pulpit view is usually the more trustworthy.

While, however, it is not my habit to write out my sermon *in extenso*, except when I have to do so for purposes of publication, I do not think that my notes would exactly be called "skeletons." When

I have selected what seems to me the best form of words for the expression of a particular and perhaps important idea, I introduce it into my notes just as I intend to deliver it; and often find that I have scarcely altered a word in the delivery of such a sentence.

To me it seems that the great secret of extempore speech lies in so arranging your notes that each particular paragraph shall by logical sequence suggest the next. It has long been my habit to draw a line between each paragraph or heading, so that the eye may the more easily distinguish each as a separate whole, and that the memory may thus be assisted. I usually glance at my notes during the reading of the lessons, and again during the singing of the hymn immediately before the sermon. Let me hope that younger brethren with either greater faith or more retentive memories may not find it needful to imitate me in this; but the use of these two opportunities leaves my mind freer from distraction to join in the more definitely devotional exercises of the service. I carefully avoid committing myself to a numerical statement of the points that I intend to consider; first, because I think that it detracts from the interest and adds to the formality of the sermon; and, second, because I am quite sure that did I thus commit myself, I should at once begin to feel nervous lest I should forget one. This actually happened to me in early ministerial life, and I had the humiliation and annoyance of being obliged to take my notes out of my Bible and, as the light was very bad, hold them up to the gas, while a horrible silence prevailed all over the church, before I could proceed with the third point promised. I would strongly recommend those who, like myself, never refer to their notes in the pulpit, to give numerical statements of heads as wide a berth as possible.

I am not a believer in the modern passion for twenty minutes' sermonettes, but I believe that I should have shown myself a much wiser man had I taken thirty-five minutes instead of forty-five as my ordinary measure. But here almost everything must depend on the character of the sermon. I heard J. B. Gough speak for one hour and three-quarters, and was only sorry when he stopped. I have heard some brethren so speak that the end was not unwelcome at the close of fifteen minutes.

With another fashion of the hour I am unable to

sympathize. Is it a reaction against the somewhat stiff and formal "application" that used to close the discourses of the Evangelical Fathers (much as a fable is usually expected to end with a moral which children are always careful not to read), that now we have no applications at all? Can this be right? Was it thus that the ancient Prophets delivered their message? Surely it is a mistake to confine the "application" to the end of the discourse; it seems to me most likely to be useful where it is least expected; but if you put no direction on your letter, you must not blame the Post Office if it be not delivered.

Let me close by saying that it is my firm conviction that preaching, like many another time-honoured institution, is "on its trial" in these iconoclastic days. It will survive the ordeal only if it proves itself fit to survive. It must show itself the fittest instrument for the moral and spiritual education of the race, or the newspaper and the magazine will oust it from its present important position. Let us endeavour to realize the responsibility that rests upon us in this respect, and use the talent that is entrusted to us to the best advantage, lest the Master have to take it from us.

# X

By the REV. ALEX. J. HARRISON, B.D.,
*Evidential Missioner of the Church Parochial Mission Society,
Lecturer of the Christian Evidence Society,
Boyle Lecturer,* 1892-1894.

A GREAT practical difficulty confronts the ordinary evidential preacher. If he dwells much upon doubt, as such, he will probably do more harm than good. The doubters will feel that their difficulties are not adequately treated, and those who have never felt or no longer feel the difficulties in question will leave the church unhelped, if not offended. Now, there is a way in which it is quite possible to help every one and hurt no one. (The reader will kindly remember that the following rules were laid down for myself, which will sufficiently account for their *brusquerie*.)

I.—In the first place, in ordinary evidential preaching, having made up your mind to banish from the pulpit, as cleanly as St. Patrick is supposed to have banished serpents from Ireland, the terms doubt, scepticism, freethinking, positivism, agnosticism, atheism, and secularism, prepare your sermon under the direct inspiration of the Holy Spirit, and with a vivid consciousness of all the difficulties that are likely to occur to those of your hearers who think. If you are not sure that you have inspiration from the Holy Spirit, pray until you are sure, and then write. Continue writing so long as the inspiration lasts, but no longer.

II.—In the second place, respect the reason of even the least thoughtful, and put into your sermon no statement that would not satisfy yourself if you were the hearer. This is important at any time, but especially when writing evidential sermons.

III.—In the third place, respect the imagination of those who listen, and, avoiding commonplace or worn-out illustrations, or, if you must use them, quickening them into new life, write down a selection from the things that come to you when your own nature is all aflame.

IV.—In the fourth place, respect the hearts of your hearers, and make no perfunctory or stereotyped appeals to a particular class of right emotions, leaving the rest unevoked, but meditate and pray over the matter until your own feeling is so intense and so uprising that it has to be held down with a strong hand.

V.—In the fifth place, respect your hearers' attention. Remember that an evidential sermon must require a certain strain on the part of the listener, and if the strain be too long continued the result may be a letting go, in which will be lost not only what at the time you are saying, but also the greater part of what you have already said. I would emphasize two points. Keep the sermon within, say, from twenty to twenty-five minutes in the morning, or from thirty to forty minutes in the evening. And do not keep any one faculty of your listener—whether reason, conscience, imagination, or emotion—solitarily active for more than two or three minutes at a time. If you cannot blend the activities of these faculties, then, at least, alternate them. Let two minutes' tension of the reason be followed by a brief relevant play of the imagination; and let the strain on the conscience be alternated by reasoned emotion or emotional reasoning. This, not that you may please, but that you may get hold and keep hold of your hearers.

VI.—In the sixth place, let your sermon be written as reverencing the Holy Spirit in your hearers. Remember that He is as truly in them that they may learn as He is in you that you may teach. Whatever, therefore, He gives to the teacher will be good for the taught, or, to give it a wider range, what He gives to the speaker will be good for the hearer.

VII.—In the seventh place, forget not that the Holy Spirit is the Spirit of Christ, and that Christ's work through any man is necessarily conditioned by his fitness for the work. Christ does and will work through you, except as your sins and ignorance hinder Him. Therefore, take care not to be ignorant and not to be sinful. To ask the Holy Spirit to make up for your deficiencies is, so far forth, to ask Him to make use, not of your brains and your heart and your conscience, but only of your tongue. Why not ask Him at once to use one of Edison's machines, and thus save you even the "labour" of talking? The Divine method is not the Holy Spirit instead of you, but the Holy Spirit in you and using you.

The promise that the Spirit of your Father will give you, in emergencies, the right thing to say is no reason for being unprepared by Him, in non-emergencies, to say the right thing. For alike the preparation of the heart—which includes all the learning faculties as well as the emotions and conscience—and the answer which the mouth makes to the questioner must be from the Divine Spirit in order to have Divine value.

VIII.—In the eighth place, remember that the mind of the Holy Spirit is not to be made known to you as if He had never said anything before. It is vanity and idleness on your part to ask Him to do over again for you individually what He has already done for you as a member of the Christian Church and as a part of the human race. The Bible, the Faith, and Science are His records of the Mind of God, and for the revelations that these contain you must go to Him in them. Remember, also, what the Divine evolution of the universe and man means, and that all things have been, are, and are becoming. Learn, therefore, genetically, historically, prophetically—looking back, around, and forward—but always interpreting the lower in the light of the higher, the temporal in the light of the eternal. Pray intensely that you may be able to see History, Literature, Poetry, Art, Education, Politics, Industry, Exploration, Colonization, Civilization, Work, and Play as movements of the Lord Jesus Christ. In other words, pray in His Spirit, until you can see His Spirit in the eyes of all men and women and children in all they have been, are, and are to be, only sin excepted.

IX.—In the ninth place, pray for such quickening as may enable you to imagine your congregation before you when writing as souls with both general and special needs. Beware of the tendency to forget the hungry in the interest you take in their food. It is right, indeed, that the food should be the very best you can prepare, provided you give it, and in such sort and in such quantity as they can take and digest. Unless you are making a deep and earnest study of human nature in its tendency to doubt and despair, do not presume to speak. Do not get into the way of making more of the doubt than of the doubter, of the despair than of the despairer. Do not look at the unbelieving man as an "unbeliever," but as a man unbelieving; do not regard the doubting man as a "doubter," but as a man doubting. Do not, in your sermons, ascribe motives, either bad or good; say nothing whatever on that subject, except in the way of prompting men to examine and know themselves; but think of all, whatever their motives, as brothers to be helped. Only do not say so. Give them the things you see they need, but do not tell them you are doing it; give them modestly, and by way of suggestion, as if your hearers were putting you under obligation in accepting your help (which, indeed, they are), not patronizingly, not dictatorially, but with unspoken and, if you can compass that, unspeakable brotherliness.

X.—In the tenth place, having trusted the Holy Spirit in the preparation of your sermon, trust Him yet more intensely in its delivery. Beware of self-suggestiveness. Shrink from that as you would from leprosy. Pray as if for your life to be saved from that. I do not mean self-conceit. As that is offensive to men as well as God, you will probably learn soon to subdue it. What I mean is, while speaking with authority and power, beware of everything that would tend to make men think that you think of it as your authority or your power. Perhaps it will help you if you remember that always the Lord Jesus Christ is one of your hearers, and the most interested of them all.

As an example of the method to be pursued in positively evidential teaching, I cannot at the moment recall anything better than Dr. R. W. Dale's recently published *Christian Doctrine*. I am not thinking of the fitness of these sermons for this or that audience; in some cases, indeed, the language used would need to be simpler still and more direct, more like the every-day speech of working-men. But as to the method, the sermons come nearer to my notion of what evidential sermons ought to be than anything else I can remember. They are not formally evidential at all; they are, what they profess to be, doctrinal; nevertheless, it is scarcely possible to read them without seeing that Dr. Dale had in mind, in composing them, the difficulties or doubts which might naturally spring up in the minds of his hearers. It is, I hope, little necessary to add that to follow Dr. Dale's example would involve, for a widely-different audience, sermons widely differing from his, but the method would in every case be the same, *i.e.* giving the positive truth in a way adapted both to those who have and those who have not, conscious difficulties or doubts on the subjects treated. It is true Dr. Dale names difficulties and doubts, while I should be disposed to leave them unnamed; yet it is so skilfully done by him that I do not suppose he ever suggests a doubt for the first time, save when it is eminently desirable to do so.

There is one piece of "worldly-wise" advice I would like to give my brethren; do not advertise your evidential sermons as evidential. If you do, you will excite at once a widespread and not altogether unjustifiable prejudice — a prejudice which will not be overcome for many a day. In my own case, of course, as I am nothing if not evidential, I have to face the prejudice; it is a necessity an "evidential missioner" cannot avoid. As a matter of prudence, and if you have any wish for promotion, avoid being specialists. Bishops and patrons generally, the Crown included, do not like specialists, and, on the whole, I think they are right. Shall I confess that of all specialists the "anti-Roman" and the "anti-infidel" professionals are to me the most terrible? Do not emphasize your evidential work, do not even call it evidential; but with all the conscience, reason, and love that are in you, with the gentleness of Christ and in the power of the Spirit, so present the truth that it shall find its way into the heads and hearts of *all* your hearers, the doubting and despairing included.

Negatively evidential sermons in the ordinary parish church, ought *not* to be given instead of the usual sermons. Our people have a right to have not only their needs but also their feelings respected, within reasonable limits. They never dictate to us what subjects we shall select, but they have a right to demand that we shall show some regard to the course of the Christian year, and to the orderly development of the whole counsel of God. To thrust upon them, therefore, a series of discourses upon the errors of other people is neither very agreeable to the best of our hearers nor very edifying to any of them. Doubtless, the "baser sort" may find it pleasant to the "old Adam" in them to learn how very unwise are the folks who do not agree with their views, but it is not good for the "New Man" in them. I should, therefore, omit from the ordinary course of teaching the *negatively* evidential sermon. But I would not omit it altogether. Let it be given on Sunday afternoons, or at any time *out* of the ordinary course, when the right people can be got together. I am not in favour of excluding women, but I would certainly exclude boys and girls, together with very young women and very young men. And I would never *urge* the people to come. On the contrary, I would have it distinctly understood that only two classes were wished for, those who have themselves difficulties or doubts, and those who wish to help those who have.

But I have not yet said what I mean by negatively evidential sermons. I mean sermons which seek to show the value of Christianity by showing the insufficiency of its alternatives. Logically, one ought to say of *all* its alternatives. Practically, this is not necessary. To win a sceptic from his particular form of scepticism is, at first sight, no guarantee that he will not adopt some other form, and it is undoubtedly true that the phases of unbelief through which one and the same man may pass are sometimes very numerous. But experience shows that, in the great majority of instances, if you can win the sceptic from *his* form of scepticism, he will not take to another form. It does not follow that he will at once come all the way to Christ, for the change might be only from Atheism or Positivism or Agnosticism to Theism; and, moreover, it is abstractly conceivable that a man might intellectually turn to Christianity itself without a corresponding change in his will and affections. But I have not found it so in actual experience. Almost—though not quite—invariably I have found the alternatives in men's minds to have one member constant. I have not found the alternatives to be Atheism or Positivism or Agnosticism, and so through all the forms of unbelief. Neither, in ninety-nine out of a hundred cases, have I found the alternatives to be the logical ones, as Theism or Atheism, &c. On the contrary, I have found the alternatives to be—

| | |
|---|---|
| Christ or Naturalism. | Christ or Spiritualism. |
| Christ or Atheism. | Christ or Freethinking. |
| Christ or Positivism. | Christ or Scepticism. |
| Christ or Pantheism. | Christ or Rationalism. |
| Christ or Agnosticism. | Christ or Secularism. |
| Christ or Deism. | Christ or Indifference. |
| Christ or Theosophy. | |

And I have known extremely few cases of a man being converted from Atheism, Positivism,

&c., to Theism and staying there. I have known hundreds of cases of men being converted to Christ at a single bound from one or other of the forms of opposition named. How is this phenomenon to be explained? Readers must judge for themselves. My own explanation is very simple. I believe the Holy Spirit to be in all men as the Spirit of Christ, and to exercise on them a guiding, though not compelling, influence in the direction of Christ. Their unbelief acts as a weight on a spring. Remove the weight, and the pressure within carries them directly to the Saviour of the world. I think the spiritual tendency of all men is towards Him Who is both Son of God and Son of Man, and, if their special obstacles be removed, all sorts of dominantly sincere seekers of righteousness and truth will at once, with a true Divine instinct, turn as readily to the Lord Jesus Christ as turns the unhindered needle to the pole. At the same time, it must not be forgotten that, whatever the special form of unbelief dealt with, the supreme appeal must be through the reason to the conscience, for Christ cannot be rightly attractive to any man, be he technically believer or unbeliever, who wills to sin.

Here are the rules which I have laid down for myself as to the negatively evidential sermons, which being given apart from morning or evening prayer may last three-quarters of an hour.

I.—In the first place, remember that the Holy Spirit who is using you as His instrument works, though He cannot yet "dwell," in the unbeliever.

II.—In the second place, acknowledge, with fearless justice, every element of truth or good which you find in any form of unbelief; and that you may find elements of good, look for them.

III.—In the third place, make due allowance for the influence of heredity and environment; and make it clear that men are responsible both for what they believe and for what they do not believe, so far as belief and unbelief are, either directly or indirectly, under their own control.

IV.—In the fourth place, while admitting that the responsibility of those to whom belief is possible, may, in some cases, be more limited than is usually supposed, show that it is yet always real, and that character and conduct have a great deal to do with belief.

V.—In the fifth place, point out that it is in vain that either believer or unbeliever says his belief or unbelief was determined by the evidence unless he can show that the evidence was: 1. Really studied. 2. Studied in the right spirit and with the right motives. And, 3. that his character and conduct, so far as voluntary, have not injuriously affected the conclusions at which he has arrived.

VI.—In the sixth place, remind your hearers that men have to give account of all deeds, whether internal or external, whether of mind or matter, and whether good or bad, done in the body, and that no man will be "punished" for anything but sin. The question which every man ought to ask himself is primarily: How far do I will *not to sin?* and then, How far is my belief or unbelief influenced by the state of my mind and heart in this respect?

VII.—In the seventh place, press home with all your power the fact that Christ alone deals adequately with the problem of redemption from sin itself, and that the question of sin's punishment is secondary to this.

VIII.—In the eighth place, make it clear that while Naturalism, Atheism, Positivism, Pantheism, Agnosticism, Deism, Theosophy, Spiritualism, Freethinking, Scepticism, Rationalism, Secularism, and even Indifference, have all elements of good which may be extracted and purified, they cannot, even in their highest forms, whether separately or combined, do anything at all towards the solution of the problem of redemption.

IX.—In the ninth place, show that except in the elements which they hold in common with Christianity, there is some excuse, but no justification for these forms of unbelief. As to the way in which this may be done, I may be permitted to refer readers to the chapter on the classification of unbelievers in my *Problems of Christianity and Scepticism*, and to the following quotation from my *Church in Relation to Sceptics*—

> Unbelief is a kind of shadow thrown by belief, and the shadow will vary according to the angle at which the belief is brought into the light. Thus Atheism is the shadow of belief in the universe, Agnosticism the shadow of belief in an omnipresent Power, Unitarianism the shadow of belief in God, Individualism the shadow of belief in Christ. What the Atheist means is that his faith is limited to the universe; what the Agnostic means is that his faith is limited to the universe *and* the omnipresent Power whose manifestation it is; what the Unitarian means is that his faith is limited to the universe as the manifestation of the omnipresent Power interpreted as God; what the Individualist means is that his faith is limited to God in Christ. The only right way of dealing with the subject is not by denunciation, but by

explanation. Put belief in the universe in the right light and the omnipresent Power appears, Atheism disappears; put belief in the omnipresent Power in the right light and God appears, Agnosticism disappears; put belief in God in the right light and the Triune Deity appears, Unitarianism disappears; put belief in Christ in the right light and the Christian Church appears, Individualism disappears.

X.—In the tenth place, while never using any weapon of unreason, while pressing home with all the intellectual energy you can the arguments and the evidence you believe to be just, never lose sight of, and always end with, the supreme problem of salvation. The interest of Christian natural religion is the existence and character of God, but the interest of Christianity is *reconciliation to God*. Bring all your powers to bear on that one point, focus all your manhood upon it; and then leave the result to the Holy Spirit Who has used you, and is at work in the unbeliever.

This chapter is already too long, yet I can hardly meet the wish of the Editor without a word or two as to my own actual method of preparation, the principles of which I have here given. I find the very first thing necessary is prayer, that I may be in the fit state of mind for writing, and very often this takes longer than all the rest of the preparation put together. I then, still praying, read over my rules, select my subject, and glance again at the rules that are most closely related to the subject. Next, I pray for spiritual insight, and for the imagined presence in the room with me of the men and women whom I wish to benefit. Then, still praying, I write as if *speaking to them*, not sermons, but chapters of books I have on hand. Sometimes I keep at this for eight or ten hours a day, sometimes for only two or three hours, sometimes weeks elapse during which I write very little, according as the pressure of other work slackens or increases. I never feel that I have the right to preach an evidential sermon until I have the substance before me in writing, and am able to form a judgment of its value as though it were some one else's. I take, still praying, from the matter before me enough for the sermon wanted, and then put it into shape for my particular purpose. When this is done I go over it as often as I find necessary to fix its points in my memory. Then I dismiss it from my mind altogether until the day comes for its delivery, when I go over it again. As the hour approaches I pray, as if for my life, for spiritual power and wisdom, and for energy of love. Then I speak, *as one who wants to save*, the sermon I have prepared, yet not fearing to say something else, if better comes, but trying still to pray always *while speaking*. For clear-headedness, for loyalty to truth, righteousness, and love, and for making points tell, there is no means so powerful as praying all the time one is preparing, and all the time one is speaking. It is *very difficult* to form the habit, but it can be done, and no one needs more to do it than the evidential preacher.

# XI

By the REV. HENRY SUTTON, M.A.,
*Vicar of Aston*

I HAVE been a preacher of missionary sermons for more years than I like to remember. It was my lot very early in my ministry to be called upon to take sermons for the C.M.S. in a country town of some importance. Nearly the whole parish belonged to one proprietor, at whose house I was a guest. A very splendid house it was; but I had not been very long there before I found that my host had only slender interest in missionary work, and looked forward to the missionary sermons of the morrow as something to be endured rather than anything else. He had received me as his guest because his wife, a very great lady who was away from home, wished him to do so. Nor did she wish it because she cared for missionary work, but because her brother, a "squarson" of considerable position, had requested her to put up the Deputation. The Curate-in-charge dined at the great house on Saturday night. He had the vaguest possible ideas about Church Societies, and evidently felt that it was absurd to expect him to know or care anything about the Church's work in foreign lands. His idea of the C.M.S. seemed to be that though it called itself a Church Society, it had very Dissenting proclivities. He was kind enough to give me one hint when he said " Good-night." It was this : " His Lordship does not like long sermons." To a young, inexperienced, nervous man (and I was very nervous in those days) all this was not encouraging. I did my best before I retired that night to improve my morning sermon. It was not to be read : I have never read a sermon in my life, but it was pretty fully written. It contained, alas! but a meagre amount of missionary information. I felt that my visit would be almost useless unless I gave some definite instruction as to the object and work of the Society for which I had come to plead.

I determined to throw over some of my pet passages, and to introduce a few facts and figures which would, at any rate, show that the need of missionary work was great, and that the results attained had been considerable. Nor did I forget to ask for help and guidance in what I felt to be a very difficult duty.

The service next day was cold and dreary. It was read in a hard, unsympathetic, drawling tone. The responses were made by an old, grey-headed clerk, who would, I suspect, have resented as an intrusion on his rights any audible participation on the part of the congregation in that portion of the service. The singing, even for a country church in those days, was slender in quantity and miserable in quality. I entered the pulpit in a dull, depressed, and despondent frame of mind. Nor was I at all encouraged by the appearance of apathetic indifference presented by the congregation at large. I say " at large," though there was " a beggarly array of empty benches," except in the pews belonging to the great house. Here and there a " poke " bonnet of a bygone age was seen, and here and there a grey-headed old man was evidently hoping to obtain a comfortable snooze. A few Sunday-school children were kept fairly quiet through fear of a long stick wielded by a stout, stern-looking person, who, I suppose, was Sunday-school superintendent.

I began with a missionary anecdote, which I told in a conversational tone with, perhaps, a suspicion of sharpness in it. A stout butler, who had folded his arms, leaned back his head, and stretched out his legs, with the evident intention of making himself as comfortable as circumstances would permit, looked up after the first few words were spoken, as much as to say, "Why, the man expects me to listen!" It was a great encouragement to me when at lunch my host asked me some questions which showed that he really wished to know more as to what the C.M.S. had been enabled actually to accomplish. It was a still greater encouragement to find not only a much larger afternoon congregation—that used to be common in the country—but an evident intention on the part of those present to listen. Here I must make a confession. My store of information was of a very limited nature. I felt that before I again went out as a "Deputation" I must make myself much more fully acquainted with "the modern Acts of the Apostles."

That early bit of experience has been fully confirmed by subsequent observation. It opened my eyes first of all to the fact that the ordinary congregation does not delight in missionary sermons; secondly, that to do one's duty in the pulpit as a missionary preacher one must have full, accurate, varied knowledge of what has, under God, been accomplished by missionary labours.

I.—Let me impress on my readers the first point just mentioned, viz. that ordinary congregations do not welcome the preacher of missionary sermons. If he happens to be a preacher with a great reputation they will, of course, be pleased to see and to hear him. But even then they will wish that his sermon may have as little missionary flavour as possible, and in a large number of cases they will be gratified.

It may be laid down as a law which admits of no exception, that where the need is deepest for clear, accurate, forcible statement of what Scripture teaches as to the duty of evangelizing the world, and what the history of modern missions proves to be the blessing which rests on the work, there the difficulty of obtaining a sympathetic hearing is greatest. Hence the need of the utmost diligence to treat this subject in such a fashion that even unwilling ears shall be made to listen.

A suitable text is of great importance. Personally

I should avoid texts which are too obviously of a missionary character. "I'll tell you what his text will be," said a young fellow one day, as he and his brother were going to a country church where a missionary sermon was to be preached. "It will either be 'Go ye into all the world, and preach the Gospel to every creature,' or 'Ask of Me, and I will give thee the heathen for thine inheritance, and the uttermost parts of the earth for thy possession,' or 'The knowledge of the glory of God shall cover the earth as the waters cover the sea,' and then we shall have all the dreary old platitudes about 'the poor heathen.' How miserable they are, how they long for the Gospel, which, of course, they care nothing about; how should they? and then a few dry statistics as to how many heathen there are, and how many converts have been made. I do hate missionary sermons." When the text was given out, it was the first of those quoted above. Neither of those boys listened much to that sermon. They were but like their elders.

The subject must be dealt with in a fresh and vigorous fashion if it is to gain attention. A text not too hackneyed is a help towards gaining the ear of a congregation. On the other hand, I very much dislike texts which must be treated in a non-natural fashion if they are to suggest missionary thoughts. As a hearer I resent an argument built up on the interpretation of a text which I feel to be forced and never intended by the sacred writer. All the time the man is preaching I keep thinking, "Yes! that is true enough *per se*, but it has nothing to do with your text." Years ago in the north of England I used to be asked, "Have you heard ——'s famous 'tail' sermon"? "No!" was my reply the first time I heard the question, "what do you mean by the 'tail sermon'?" "Why, wherever —— goes for the —— he preaches at least once from the words 'Take it by the tail,' and a very good sermon he preaches from that peculiar text. People always remember the text whatever else they forget." No doubt; but that sort of artifice does not commend itself to my mind. It is a good thing that the text should be remembered when it suggests thoughts germane to one's subject; it is a good thing that attention should be awakened by one's text, but unless attention is rewarded by what follows not much has been gained. Whilst I would, therefore, eschew texts which are too obviously of a missionary character, I would still more eschew those which are fanciful and calculated rather to surprise by their ingenuity than to instruct by their appositeness.

The Acts of the Apostles more than any other book of the Bible is a treasure-house of missionary texts. In using that book the preacher will almost of necessity compare it with the Epistles of St. Paul. He will thus be enabled to show how missionary work was done in Apostolic times; how difficulties were overcome; and what, in my judgment, is of supreme importance, he will be enabled to prove, to use a term for which I have no love, the solidarity of spiritual work in all places and in all ages.

If I may venture to illustrate my meaning by actual examples I would take one or two favourite topics. In Acts xiii. 2 we read, "Separate me Barnabas and Saul for the work whereunto I have called them." Naturally one asks oneself where the Apostles were when this command was given. How had they been led to Antioch? We see how naturally, and yet how clearly, under God's guidance the two great missionaries had been brought to that city. Nay, more, we learn from Acts xi. that the foundation of the Church at Antioch was due to persecution at Jerusalem. There was nothing miraculous in the whole matter. Persecuted Christians bear witness to their Lord, and He blesses their word.

The duty which devolves on all Christians to bear witness to what God has done for their souls through Christ can be briefly yet powerfully brought home as there is passed in review the work of those men " of Cyprus and Cyrene, who, when they were come to Antioch, spake unto the Greeks" [margin, Authorized Version], "preaching the Lord Jesus."

The interest felt in the infant Church at Antioch by the comparatively small, poor, and persecuted mother Church of Jerusalem manifested by sending to Antioch Barnabas, "the son of exhortation" (or consolation), may well be contrasted with the indifference too often shown by Christians in England with regard to the triumphs of the Gospel in heathen lands in our own times.

The duty of fostering, developing, and putting on a firm basis an infant Church by bringing in workers who have the needed gifts for such a task, is easily emphasized when the action of Barnabas in bringing Saul from Tarsus to Antioch to help him in his work there is noted.

Once more picturing Antioch, its magnificence, its importance as a great pleasure city, to which men from many lands, speaking many tongues, professing many religions, were gathered together, it is impossible to help asking what most Christians of to-day, who are not yet missionary enthusiasts, would have thought about the wisdom of sending away from such a city, where their work was so needed, the best of all the ministers of the Gospel then at Antioch.

It needs no great gift of imagination to picture the smallness, weakness, insignificance, from the mere worldly point of view, of the work already done at Antioch. Nor will a congregation be slow to see that looking at the question from the point of view of worldly prudence, nothing could seem more disastrous to the interests of the Church at Antioch than obedience to the bidding of the Holy Ghost. But all Christian people, and even worldly people, will admit that disobedience to the command on the part of the Apostles themselves, or on the part of the Church at Antioch, must have meant a withdrawal of Divine blessing from that Church.

It is quite easy to show, further, that the difficulties which met the Apostles in their first missionary journey, and the successes they achieved have been paralleled in the history of modern Missions, whilst if it is thought needful to apologize for introducing missionary details to the notice of a Christian congregation, the action of the Apostles on their return to Antioch may well be pleaded. Their action in "calling the Church together and rehearsing all that God had done with them, and how He had opened the door of faith to the Gentiles," is full justification for giving details of missionary work to Christians to-day. In trying to show that the call to missionary work in our day is as real as that given to the Church at Antioch, it is, of course, necessary to remind one's hearers that to know God's will we must read His Word, and carefully consider the circumstances of the age in which we live.

Some knowledge of the openings for missionary work, and of the blessing now given is needful for effective illustration of this point.

Once more. I have found it interesting and

useful to draw attention to the teaching of one of St. Paul's Epistles, taken as a whole, on the missionary subject. The First Epistle to the Thessalonians lends itself readily to such treatment. The work at Thessalonica presents many points of resemblance to that done in modern times, both as to its successes and its disappointments. Men there "turned from idols to serve the living and true God." They "received the Word in much affliction, yet with joy of the Holy Ghost"; they "received the Word not as the Word of man, but as it is in truth, the Word of God." From them "sounded forth the Word of the Lord."

In dealing with such a subject, very great care is needed in the illustrations which are used. They must not be left to the inspiration of the moment. Mere vague, indefinite declamation as to the numbers who in modern times have forsaken their idols, produces no good effect. A contrast between Sierra Leone in the early days of Mission-work there and Sierra Leone to-day, or an account of what has taken place at Lagos, on the Niger, or at Abbeokuta, in repudiation of idolatry, cannot fail to be impressive. The records of modern missions are full of illustrations of persecution joyfully borne for Christ's sake. Africa—both west and east—India, China, Japan, North-west America, all supply such illustrations. It seems to me of the utmost importance first to select carefully what one means to tell, and then to take great pains how one tells one's story. An old Methodist minister used to say, " Leave whatever other parts of your sermon you like unwritten, but write your illustrations." Excellent advice; one ought to have no doubt about names, places, dates. It gives great confidence to the hearers when these are given with precision.

I have already dwelt on the unwillingness of people to listen to missionary sermons. I am pretty sure that that unwillingness arises partly from scepticism about missionary facts. That scepticism is nourished by the manner in which such facts are often given. The use of " I think," failure to give precise details, which are capable of verification, the use of fine adjectives where facts alone are needed, have, I am sure, done much to inspire doubt about stories which are absolutely true.

Here I must enter a protest against the terrible

inaccuracy, to call it by no harsher term, which characterizes some preachers and speakers when telling so-called facts. It does a mint of mischief. It is very often due to mere idleness. The main fact is often true; but it is hid beneath a mass of details which have grown around it as it has passed from lip to lip.

If in doubt do not dare to use the incident, however telling it may seem; where it is possible, go to the fountain-head for information. When you have verified your story tell it with confidence, and give, where possible, names of persons, of places, and the exact time at which the incident occurred. This, I know, is not always possible; but when, for sufficient reason, such details are suppressed, say why you keep them back. It is one thing to tell a story, it is another to gain for it credence. If you do not secure this latter point your story is worse than useless.

We cannot err much if we make Scripture the foundation for all our teaching on the missionary subject.

I have found it useful sometimes to dwell upon the wonderful way in which certain events in the life of St. Paul which seemed most unlikely to do so were overruled to the furtherance of the Redeemer's kingdom. Take, for example, the events which led up to his being sent as a prisoner to Rome. In the vision vouchsafed to St. Paul when the Lord appeared and said "Be of good cheer, Paul, for as thou hast borne witness of Me at Jerusalem so shalt thou also bear witness at Rome," we see (1) that man's extremity is God's opportunity; (2) that God's purposes are often wrought out in what seem to us most unlikely ways; (3) that the greatest blessing to a heart right with God is the promise of being permitted to do more work for Him. But in dealing with such a subject it must not be forgotten that modern instances are absolutely necessary if the object of the missionary preacher is to be attained. He must, therefore, be able to bring forward authentic cases from the records of missionary history, to prove that God does now give to His servants in their darkest hours the very comfort they need. Bishop Hannington's life affords more than one illustration of this fact.

The second point is abundantly illustrated in the history of the English in India. Clive and Warren Hastings are unconscious instruments for making it possible to proclaim Christ in India. The slave trade, with all its horrors, is a link in the chain of providential circumstance which brings the Gospel to Africa. British love of travel is overruled to the same end. A Revolution in Japan—apparently without any bearing on the religious history of the world—opens up the "land of the rising sun" to missionary effort.

Any one who knows what missionaries have done, the sacrifices which some persons at home have made for the extension of the Redeemer's kingdom, the way in which successful effort always means a call to more exertion, can readily prove the third point. It lends itself also to personal appeal as to our own spiritual condition. I take it that no missionary sermon is what it ought to be where such appeal is wanting. I never heard Samuel Hasell preach, though I often listened with pleasure and profit to his masterly speeches. I have been told, however, by excellent judges, that a sermon of his on Acts xiv. 21-23 always produced a great impression on those who heard it. His special object in that sermon was to show that missionaries to-day do just what Paul and Barnabas did. There is the Evangelistic work represented in the words, "They preached the Gospel in that city" [Derbe] "and taught many." There is the work of building up, seen in the words, "They returned again to Lystra and to Iconium and Antioch." There is the fact that now, as then, there is sure to be opposition to the Gospel and persecution of those who become followers of Christ—"We must through much tribulation enter into the kingdom of God." And more important, perhaps, than anything else is the thought that now, as then, a native ministry must be one great object of missionary work—"And when they had ordained them elders in every Church, and had prayed with fasting, they commended them to the Lord, on whom they believed." It is astonishing how ignorant people in general are about the number and quality of the native clergy and native lay workers in the Mission-field. Nothing interests an ordinary congregation more than information, carefully given, about native workers. I have found it effective when mentioning the name of a native clergyman to spell the name, and to add that the name will be found in the *Clergy List*. The more outlandish the name the more need is there to take care that people really know what it is; and the more impression is produced by connecting it with our English clergy. The sceptical spirit of which I spoke earlier in this chapter can only be exorcized by the utmost circumstantiality of statement. When people hear that they can find in *Crockford* the name of the Rev. Tushtu Chandra Tarafdar, of Goginda, Krishnagar, India, and of the Rev. Heta Tarawhiti, of Waikato, South Auckland, New Zealand, and of the Rev. Henry Wright Duta, Uganda, the Rev. Ngoi Kaik-Ki, the College, Fuh-chow, China—they begin to believe that these persons exist. They no longer seem vague, unreal, the figment of clerical fancy.

If the preacher can give the life-history of any or all whose names he thinks it well to mention, so much the better; but he has accomplished something when he has brought it home to the average common-sense, practical Englishman that reproductive work is going on in the Mission-field. Not unnaturally the ordinary Englishman, even when he is an earnest Christian, resents the idea that the whole world is to be evangelized by Europeans. When he learns that already there are self-supporting, self-extending, and, to some extent, self-governing Churches which have been planted within the present century, he begins to feel that missionary effort is not a wild Quixotic affair, but a matter that demands and deserves the active aid of all true followers of Christ.

I am quite aware that some of my readers will be inclined to think that a good deal of what I have said is suited rather to the missionary speech than to the missionary sermon. But we must remember that for far the larger part of most congregations the missionary speech might as well never be delivered. It is heard by the select few. It is heard, for the most part, by persons already interested in Missions. The subject will never have its right place in the affections of our people unless it is treated in the pulpit with some adequate degree of detail.

I have had in mind the preacher of missionary sermons who goes as a stranger to a parish, who has the opportunity of preaching one, two, or three sermons on the Sunday. I hold that in such a case the sermon must not be a mere missionary speech, though it must contain missionary information.

Where are preachers to find suitable information? There is no royal road to learning. One must be content to read missionary reports, missionary periodicals, and, above all, missionary biographies, if one is to be well furnished for the task of preaching missionary sermons. The missionary literature of to-day is so interesting and abundant that there ought to be no difficulty in finding a sufficient amount of suitable information. For a man pressed for time, I know nothing to equal *Missionary Facts and Figures*, by the Rev. J. D. Mullins. There is an amazing amount of valuable matter compressed in the nine small pages of that tract. For making use of missionary information no plan, in my judgment, equals that of illustrating each part of one's sermons by facts as one proceeds from point to point. A plan that may be adopted with success, at times, is to begin with a few facts and figures of a striking character. Then to deal with one's text entirely from the spiritual point of view, taking care to finish with an application which shall bring the mind of the hearer back to the special object of the sermon. If figures are given at all it should be sparingly, and not at the end of the sermon. I take for granted that, as a general rule, the missionary sermon will not be read. I know that there are preachers who can manage a manuscript so cleverly as to afford all the ease, comfort, and accuracy of the written, with the fire and force of the so-called extempore, sermon. This, however, is rare. But, whether a man reads or not, he should, in my judgment, write. The pen is a great aid to clearness of thought, accuracy of statement, and brevity. Oh! the weariness of listening to words, words, words, with a minimum of meaning. I would rather have a slow laboured utterance than the easy flow of talk which leaves no impression. My father used to tell with gusto how a man in our village said of a certain preacher, "It takes a deal of fetching up; but it is very good when it does come." That is more than can be said of all preachers. I am no advocate for learning sermons by heart. I use the pen myself because I can think best pen in hand, and because I find that I can put more matter into my sermons, and be more sure that I keep close to my point when I write than when I speak or preach without having previously written.

When I have departed from my custom of only preaching after having written, I have nearly always regretted it. I had one Saturday night talked with my host, who was a very able preacher, about sermon preparation, and had found that he strongly approved of writing, even though one did not mean to read. On Sunday morning there was something in one of the lessons which seemed to me to fit exactly certain rather exciting matters of current interest in the Mission-field. I threw over my sermon, took my text from the lesson, and managed to bring in my recent information. "You had not written that sermon, I think," said my host; and I felt that I had made a mistake. I might almost equally well have brought in the only part of that sermon that was of any value into the one I had prepared.

Here, indeed, is an advantage possessed by the missionary preacher. He can adapt his sermon to circumstances; he can leave out what evidently fails to interest; he can improve his sermon each time it is delivered. In this way he will learn what Whitefield meant by saying, "A sermon begins to be good when I have preached it forty times." As a matter of experience, I have always found that after a few repetitions the sermon became shorter. Inasmuch as I never learned by heart, I could never preach a sermon exactly the same twice over. That does not apply to missionary anecdotes. I try to tell them as briefly, pointedly, and truthfully as possible ; and, having done my best to tell a story well, I do not change my mode of telling it. This I have found to be the case with the best missionary advocates I have had the happiness of hearing. Unless a man has a wonderful gift of putting well, on the spur of the moment, information he has just received, he ought never to attempt to weave into his sermon fact or incident which he has not had time to assimilate thoroughly.

The motto of the missionary preacher must be " Prayer and pains." Study God's Word with earnest prayer, study the new Acts of the Apostles with prayer no less earnest, and then do your very best to present the principles you have gleaned from Revelation, and the facts you have learned from the records of missionary labours in the clearest, most concise, most convincing manner. Speak naturally, simply, earnestly. Let it be clear that you are master of your subject, that you regard it as of supreme importance, that you are full of faith as to the ultimate reign of Christ in the world, and then the congregation will listen as to one who has lifted what was once to them an uninteresting topic to a loftier level, and, what is far better, will feel that they must have their share in carrying out their Lord's parting command to His Church.

THE END.